School Library Makerspaces

School Library Makerspaces
Grades 6–12

Leslie B. Preddy

John Read Middle School
486 Redding Road
Redding, Connecticut 06896

LIBRARIES UNLIMITED

AN IMPRINT OF ABC-CLIO, LLC

Santa Barbara, California • Denver, Colorado • Oxford, England

Library of Congress Cataloging-in-Publication Data

Preddy, Leslie.
    School library makerspaces : grades 6-12 / Leslie B. Preddy.
        pages cm.
    ISBN 978-1-61069-494-0 (pbk.) — ISBN 978-1-61069-495-7 (ebook) 1. School libraries—Activity programs—Handbooks, manuals, etc. 2. Middle school libraries—Activity programs—Handbooks, manuals, etc. 3. High school libraries—Activity programs—Handbooks, manuals, etc. 4. Library orientation—Aids and devices—Handbooks, manuals, etc. 5. Educational technology—Handbooks, manuals, etc. I. Title.
    Z675.S3P743 2013
    027.8—dc23   2013025274

ISBN: 978-1-61069-494-0
EISBN: 978-1-61069-495-7

17 16 15 14 13   1 2 3 4 5

This book is also available on the World Wide Web as an eBook.
Visit www.abc-clio.com for details.

Libraries Unlimited
An Imprint of ABC-CLIO, LLC

ABC-CLIO, LLC
130 Cremona Drive, P.O. Box 1911
Santa Barbara, California 93116-1911

This book is printed on acid-free paper ∞

Manufactured in the United States of America

For my mother, Rochelle Elaine Roche Burton,
who is the creative heart and soul of our family
and my inspiration.

To my father, Ronald Carl Burton,
who is the advisor and mentor of our family
and whom I strive to grow up to be.

And to my husband, Jim,
who is my best friend, my champion,
my cheerleader, and my personal hero.

For my kids,
love you to the moon and back - olive juice.

Contents

Preface

The library makerspace revolution is forward thinking and progressive, yet brings us back to our country's historical ingenuity roots of basement tinkerers, hobbyists, and artisans.

The role of the school librarian and the school library within the school community are ever changing as the needs of the community changes and human thinking, interaction, and learning processes evolve. As I look back on two decades as a school librarian, not only has the *look* of the school library facility changed multiple times, but so have my responsibilities as I adapt what I do and how I serve the needs of my patrons to better fit their requirements and interests as they also continually change to fit the new world in which we live. This is what makes being a school librarian so interesting and, honestly, so much down-right fun. What a great profession! Where else is one able to have a fresh, new start annually; get to reinvent the role frequently; see the influence of making a difference in the face of appreciative and engaged students, staff and parents; and all without a career change?

Now the makerspace philosophy is coming to school libraries, which is an exciting paradigm shift in modality. Treat the new makerspace as you would any new endeavor. Be realistic. Start with your current skills, talents, and comfort level, and expand from there. The school library makerspace revolution is a confusing one. It is confusing because there are so many ideas for what it is, could, or should be. It is important to keep in mind that there is no right or wrong way for school library makerspace design or programming. Every library makerspace is different because every library, community, librarian, and patron base is different. Some have a technology-tinker focus, some have a science twist, while others are hobby and craft-based, but there is no right or wrong. There is no must-do or must have. The only goal is to encourage thinking and provide experiential knowledge, to enable problem-solving, and hands-on doing. Doing what feels right makes coming to work fun, draws the interest and participation of patrons, and makes the school library *the* destination. Start with what is familiar, comfortable, affordable, and expand the repertoire from that foundation.

Introduction

"I love it when your area is hopping with kids from wall to wall doing a variety of activities and using every space!"
—David Rohl, Principal, Perry Meridian Middle School

School libraries have always been a destination of thinking and learning, but now they are also the destination of doing, creating, and producing. The purpose of this resource is to share with school librarians concepts and resources to create a school library makerspace on a budget with some kick-start, genuine creativity. The library becomes a place to reinvent the learning and doing and creating for the inventor, artist, craftsman, industrial technologist, hobbyist, storyteller, cook, tinkerer, dreamer, and do-it-yourselfer. A maker organization for adults is different than a makerspace for public libraries, which is different than a makerspace for school libraries. A true maker organization for adults is a collaborative environment of idea sharing, problem-solving, constructivism, crafting, and engineering, with a heavy dose of tech gadgets. Although it is realistic and feasible in some school environments to build this sort of community within the school, this is often expensive and the technology-engineering learning curve is a venture which requires more time, flexibility, and leadership focus than is reasonable given the time frame of a school year.

Create your own, affordable, realistic makerspace to fit within the available library space, patrons' interests, and the library community's learning needs, values, and finances. This resource is about developing a center which brings together creativity, engagement, and traditional craftsmanship with an alternative, updated twist. Projects found in this book include a focus on upcycling, reinventing traditional crafts, making a difference in the community, repurposing books and periodicals, STEM (science, technology, engineering, mathematics), silly and simple, and make-and-take activities, with an emphasis on thinking, creating, sharing, and growing.

Use this book to help guide your thinking, planning, learning, and implementation. The makerspace concept may have its challenges such as: space; required adult supervision; the expertise of expert mentors for some projects; limited funding; safety concerns; scheduling of projects; and systematically aligning local, state, and national goals and standards to projects and experiences. Overcome obstacles one at time, take a deep breath, and take the plunge into making the school library the hub of experiential learning. If you are a makerspace enthusiast, but limited by one or all of the design issues, Chapter 1 will guide you through how to dip into the revolution without needing a large investment of time, space, or money. Peruse the pages following Chapter 2 to be inspired by project ideas which can be adapted or immediately implement as-is in your own makerspace. For delving deeper into other makerspace experiences and technologies, further project ideas and inspiration can be found in Appendix 3.

Although a community or public library makerspace is very constructivist, this resource leans more toward the crafty and creative; allowing for the development of some traditional, basic physical skills with a dash of fun, ingenuity, problem-solving, and thinking. It is intended to be student centered with activities ranging from a simple activity completed in just minutes, to others which will require learning new skills and take the attention stamina of days or weeks to complete. Some are individual accomplishments; others are intended to develop teamwork and collaborative thinking skills.

Once a level of comfort has been reached, branch out and expand the makerspace to incorporate maker mentors, makers-in-residence, and more complicated, technical ventures, or craft and trade skills beyond your current repertoire. Appendix 2 includes local and national maker events and Appendix 4 is an annotated list of maker communities and resources.

Remember the maker philosophy that there is no wrong way of doing things and what is important is the trying, the doing, learning from failures, and figuring out a new way of doing.

And most importantly, enjoy!

The School Library Makerspace

A makerspace is an exciting opportunity for school libraries to take that next evolutionary step toward making the library a destination, instead of a fly-by stop. Chris Anderson, author of *Makers: The New Industrial Revolution*, argues that America is currently in the clutches of a new industrial revolution of inventors and entrepreneurs successfully designing and producing on a smaller scale of micro-manufacturing, making it possible for each of us to be an aspiring creative genius and a success story

(Anderson 2012). A makerspace is a community destination where students—sometimes alongside staff, parents, and mentors—can create, problem solve, and develop skills, talents, thinking, and mental rigor. Envision the DIY Network meets the hands-on learning philosophy of a children's museum, but right there in the school library. What could be more exciting than seeing, doing, and thinking in a place where knowledge, information, and inquiry were born and encouraged?

Makerspaces in School Libraries

The four key components to inquiry, lifelong learning, and the American Association of School Librarians (AASL) *Standards for the 21st-Century Learner* are think, create, share, and grow. Examine these four words, simple yet complex learning and thinking concepts. They are integral to the newest advancement in school libraries and school librarianship. A library makerspace exists on the same founding principles as the national standards for student learning: thinking, creating, sharing,

and growing. It is a place to develop guided experiences to build foundational skills and facilitate independent making opportunities.

A makerspace is a place for students to be active learners. A safe place to creatively construct, problem solve, and question current thinking and ways of doing. It is a place to build cognitive, kinesthetic, and social skills. Through makerspace activities students build core skills: dexterity, thinking, problem solving, following step-by-step instructions, group dynamics, patience, endurance, and the ability to try new things. From guided learning experiences, students grow, develop skills, become inspired, and become more independent building on their personal interests, and becoming inspired to try new things in the flexible makerspace environment. When envisioning a makerspace, think how exciting it would be to blend industrial technology, art, family and consumer science, crafting, science, digital media construction, engineering, tinkering, and recycling into one space. Consider how it might look!

Facility

My mother is a crafty person. Among her talents is quilting, so she has a keen spatial eye. She often expresses the importance of a space needing to meet its utilitarian need but with a touch of ambiance. Look about your library facility and consider how it could be re-arranged or the space re-distributed to accommodate a unique stationery or mobile makerspace within the library. Create a space that is human centered in design and conducive to project-based thinking and learning.

Reinvent the library space; stand in the center of the facility and make a turn, looking all around. Could books or storage be consolidated and some shelves or cabinets be removed to make room for the makerspace or even repurposed for use in the new space? Is there an underutilized nook or room near the library? Is there a space which was perfect and fitting for the school's needs and patrons a few years ago, but now lays dormant? If unable to be inspired, invite somebody you trust implicitly to look at the space with you and help brainstorm possibilities.

Make the space distinctive through decorations or signage or both. Consider the purpose and budget while creating and constructing the design area. There should be enough space for the activities supplies, instructions, people's work space, and project storage. If the space, patronage, and community allow for autonomous productivity and activity, there should be enough supplies laid out to get through the day without direct physical instruction or limited supervision. Provide seating or standing space for the maximum number of patrons who can safely use the space at one time. Allow for table or countertop room for each person to work. Deliver adequate lighting and electrical outlets.

Storage space for supplies and projects in progress could be portable or permanent. Nearby shelving could be converted to cubbies. Utilize plastic crates, tubs, or recycle plastic restaurant take-away containers, which could be used for storing projects in progress. It is important to have a system in place to store an active project in between visits by a patron. This keeps the project protected and intact. In order to complete a particular makerspace activity, it may require multiple visits due to time requirements or the type of event requiring wait time for drying, setting, or complexity. Keeping patrons' in-progress projects protected may be logical and simple, yet imperative.

Keep the area as uncomplicated as possible. This would make it easy to clean after a day of active use and easy to convert from one makerspace event to staging for the next activity.

Large whiteboards or painting walls with whiteboard paint are a way for thought sharing, quick advice, fun communication, and the building of a collective conceptual framework. If that is not possible, consider other solutions. Potential creative solutions could be covering walls with removable butcher paper or using a portable chalkboard, whiteboard, or bulletin board.

Cloud computing is useful for contributing to the common knowledge and communicating thinking and doing to others involved in the project. This is especially useful for complex tasks and for groups who may never or infrequently be able to work in the makerspace at the same time. Through the cloud, students, and even mentors, can work in tandem, without proximity hindering thinking, and learning, and doing. Through the cloud, a group can participate in the thinking and doing without worrying about coordinating schedules or always being face-to-face to work, think, do, and create together.

Money and Budgets

Creative budgeting and materials hunting is needed for long-term success. If possible, set aside a percentage of the library's annual supply or programming budget. Administration may also be receptive to helping with the venture, especially once they see the unique activities and active thinking going on in the makerspace. Write a one-page, bulleted proposal explaining purpose, need, goals, a brief outline of the plan, and specific start-up and ongoing budget needs. Further sway the administration by including a tentative schedule of makes and the skills and academic standards met through each activity. This idea will be much more receptively received if the proposal includes attempts and efforts to seek outside funding to help with start-up costs and creative solutions for ongoing supply needs. Once a clear and thoughtful proposal has been prepared, make an appointment and share the plan with administration.

Discounts: Contact local hobby, home improvement, craft, and technology businesses for non-profit discount programs available to teachers, schools, libraries, or non-profits.

Donations: Contact local recycle centers, hobby and craft organizations, clubs, and stores for material and equipment donations. This should be done at point of need. As soon as a particular make is considered, make a list of the start-up supplies needed and who might help with donations. For example, when needing beeswax, might a local bee-keeper be willing to donate or reduce cost if you explain who you are and the need?

Grants: Grants for equipment or materials may also be obtained from local businesses and local, state, and national philanthropic organizations. For example, many local McDonald's sponsor annual Mac grants for educators. Start-up materials could mean starting the makerspace or starting a new skill in the makerspace, which require new equipment, tools, or supplies, like a sewing machine or littleBits.

Partnerships: Contact local guilds, clubs, and other organizations related to the specific makerspace activity needing sponsorship for a monetary or material donation. For example, contact the local Leather Guild before beginning a make on leathercrafting.

Maker Fees: If necessary, charge a minimal fee to cover the cost for more expensive makes, or to cover the expense of one specific supply required for the make. Only charge the student for the cost of the make if they are permitted to take home what they create; but if using, for example, ProtoSnap in a make, then require the student to return the ProtoSnap parts, and do not charge a fee. If including a make fee, place the fee on a sliding scale so those who cannot afford to pay are not restricted from participating.

Guided Instruction

It is important for patrons to have creative freedoms in this space, but even with artistic flexibility, guidance is needed to learn core skills for any task. Students learn through a range of text, visual, auditory, and kinesthetic clues. Model ethical behavior. Include copyright and credit within the training material for each activity, even if it is just an "inspired by" reference. Whenever possible, include students in the development and creation of instructional materials.

The school library makerspace projects advance in stages from learning and building knowledge through a guided task, to an independent challenge, to fully independent and self-directed objective.

Learning and Building Knowledge

Before students can become independent, they need guidance, direction, and training. Many times students need these basic experiences to broaden their horizons and learn about things they otherwise may not even know exist. Always create the project first in order to better know the task. By going through the make yourself, it is easier to understand the make, its pitfalls, errors in initial instructions, missing supplies, missing steps to consider, and even substitutions or adaptations. Display examples of the final products for the current makerspace activity. Exhibit instructional signs or papers; include both images and text in the how-to step-by-step. Provide books, videos, blogs, websites, and other resources to further expand the depth of learning and foundation of knowledge. If the school's technology allows, expand the visual experience by creating or locating how-to videos to play on a continuous loop on a video compatible digital picture frame, laptop, or DVD player. Share in a format familiar to students, or even required by the school, the activity's objective and local, state, or national standards being met.

Independent Challenges

Once a student has established basic skills through a guided project, he is ready for an independent challenge. In a challenge task, students take what has already been learned to further develop related skills and deepen knowledge through completing an independent challenge presented by the makerspace coordinator. The challenge is phrased as a task with a final goal in mind, as well as some recommended, preliminary resources. From there, it is up to the student to work out what steps are necessary to successfully take their learning to the next level and successfully complete the make.

Self-Directed Experiment

In a self-directed task, the student is ready to set an autonomous goal based on what she has learned and where she is inspired to take her learning. Learning will continue through personal inquiry, establishing a goal, developing a plan of action and timeline, and making a final product. Through a self-directed make student's problem-solve, troubleshoot, gain a sense of independence and confidence, stretch their creativity, and build on previous learning and experiences to expand their own personal learning. Optimally, they contribute to the greater good of the community by sharing their self-directed inspirations and creations with the maker community.

Pathfinders

Pathfinders have been a staple of information communication in libraries for decades and are still an excellent concept for sharing, whether web-based or a paper copy. Create a webpage, bookmark, flyer, or index-sized card mini-pathfinder for patrons to use during the make and to take away for further scholarship. Include recommendations for books, websites, community places, events, and organizations participants can go to for further learning and related activities to do on their own and grow from a novice to an experienced maker on that topic.

Learning Standards

Local, state, and national standards for creativity, productivity, thinking, learning, contributing, and inquiry are met through makerspace activities. AASL Standards for the 21st-Century Learner, Common Core College and Career Readiness Anchor Standards, and STEM are important in the development of lifelong learners, productive thinkers, and are integrated into the thinking and doing of a school library makerspace.

AASL Standards for the 21st-Century Learner

Think

Thinking includes learning from the expertise and experience of others. As the more technically complicated makes get under way, students will need to recognize when they've hit a roadblock and need help from those with more understanding and experiences with the task. If a concept or solution is found by someone else or through research, credit should be given to that individual or resource. Integral to the library makerspace philosophy is the sharing of knowledge, experience, and solutions.

For full text of the AASL Standards for the 21st-Century Learner, please visit http://www.ala.org/aasl/guidelines andstandards/learningstandards/standards

School Library Makerspace Pathfinder

A School Library Makerspace is a destination of thinking, learning, doing, creating, and producing; where students are makers who think, create, share, and grow. It is a place to reinvent old ideas with new conceptual frameworks, utilize advancements in thinking and doing, and investigate and construct a hybrid of fine arts, sciences, crafts, industrial technologies, foods, inventions, shop class, textiles, hobbies, community pay-it-forward, digital media, upcycling, and DIY concepts. Every library makerspace is unique but all intersect with the underlying philosophy to encourage thinking, experimenting, problem-solving, experiential knowledge, and hands-on doing.

LIBRARY MAKERS, MAKERSPACES and THINK TANKS

Fayetteville Free Library Fab Lab <http://fflib.org/make>
A groundbreaking public library makerspace.

Library Makers: Hands-On Learning for All Ages <http://librarymakers.blogspot.ca/>
A blog dedicated to hands-on, person-to-person learning in the library setting.

Maker Cookbook <https://docs.google.com/a/perryschools.org/document/d/1lyYoqNZUI6j45LrXV8Go86DVcr6Xm7r7nIk8UvNiNWU/edit?usp=sharing&pli=1>
A place for librarians to contribute ideas for makerspace activities.

Mentor Makerspaces <http://mentor.makerspae.com/>
A community built just for schools and teachers interested in makerspaces.

MIT Media Labs: High-Low Tech Group <http://hlt.media.mit.edu/>
The MIT Media Lab research group which focuses on the integration of high and low tech.

Mt. Elliott Makerspace <http://www.mtelliottmakerspace.com/>
Developed to meet stated goals through state focus areas and particular skills development and themed workshops.

Westport Public Library Maker Space. <http://www.westportlibrary.org/services/maker-space>
A family friendly public library makerspace, often includes the creation of very large group makes.

WORDS to KNOW

3D Printing
Apps
Arduino
Cloud Computing
Coding
Creative Commons
Digital Badge
DIY Couture
E-Textiles
Fabrication
Instructable
Make and Take
Maker Faire
MakerBot®
Micro-Manufacturing
Open Source
Prototype
Soft Circuit
STEM
Storyboard
Upcycling
Wearables

ARTICLES and WEB RESOURCES

- ALA TechSource. Archive of Makerspaces. Webinar series, 2012-2013. <http://www.alatechsource.org/search/node/archive%20of%20makerspaces>
  A four part webinar series, *Makerspaces: A New Wave of Library Service*. Each webinar spotlights a different library makerspace and their interpretation and focus for facilities, programming, mission, and philosophy.

- American Libaries magazine. January/February 2013 issue. (American Library Association). <http://americanlibrariesmagazine.org/features/02062013/manufacturing-makerspaces>
  Much of this issue is dedicated to the library makerspace revolution and aiding librarians with a basic understanding and resources.

- Catalano, Frank. "Want to Start a Makerspace at School? Tips to Get Started", KQED, February 12, 2013. <http://blogs.kqed.org/mindshift/2013/02/want-to-start-a-makerspace-at-school-tips-to-get-started/>

- "The Makings of Makerspaces" 3 part series, Library Journal (via The Digital Shift). <http://www.thedigitalshift.com/2012/10/public-services/the-makings-of-maker-spaces-part-1-space-for-creation-not-just-consumption/>
  Moving from the era collection to the evolution of community based programming.

- "Libraries, Hackspaces and E-waste: how libraries can be the hub of a young maker revolution", American Library Association, February 28, 2013. <http://www.ilovelibraries.org/libraries-hackspaces-and-e-waste-how-libraries-can-be-hub-young-maker-revolution>
  Enthusiastic shout out for the purposeful need for library makerspaces.

- Britton, Lauren. "A Fabulous Labaratory: The Makerspace at Fayetteville Free Library." Public Libraries. July/August 2012. (American Library Association) <http://publiclibrariesonline.org/2012/10/a-fabulous-labaratory-the-makerspace-at-fayetteville-free-library/>

- "Talking Points: Museums, Libraries, and Makerspaces", Institute of Museum and Library Services, September 2012. <http://www.imls.gov/assets/1/AssetManager/Makerspaces.pdf>
  The importance and support of STEM and Makerspaces from the federal library and museum grant making federal agency.

IDEAS FOR THE MAKE-ing

GET INSPIRED

John Seely Brown on Motivating Learners (Big Thinkers Series). Stephen Brown. March 6, 2013. <http://www.edutopia.org/john-seely-brown-motivating-learners-video?utm_source=facebook&utm_medium=pos&utm_campaign=video-seelytinker>.

BOOKS and MAGAZINES

Anderson, Chris. Makers: The New Industrial Revolution. (Crown Business, 2012)

MAKE Magazine (Maker Media)
The leading print and online magazine for makers.

Makerspace Team. Makerspace Playbook DRAFT. <http://makerspacedoncom.files.worpress.com/2012/04/makerspaceplaybook-201204.pdf>

Montano, Mark. The Big-Ass Book of Bling (Gallery Books, 2012);The Big-Ass Book of Crafts 2 (Gallery Books, 2011), The Big-Ass Book of Home Décor (Stewart Tabori & Chang, 2010), The Big-Ass Book of Crafts (Simon Spotlight Entertainment, 2008),

Thompson, Jason. Playing with Books: The Art of Upcycling, Deconstructing, and Reimagining the Book. (Quarry Books, 2010)

Upcycle Magazine <http://www.upcyclemagazine.com/>

THINKING and DOING

DIY <https://diy.org/skills>

Howtoons <http://www.howtoons.com/>
Instructables <http://www.instructables.com/>

Purdue University: Indiana 4-H Youth Development
    <http://www.four-h.purdue.edu/projects/index.cfm>

YouTube Channels

eHow™ Arts and Crafts
<http://www.youtube.com/user/eHowArtsAndCrafts>

Geek & Sundry: TableTop <http://www.youtube.com/user/geekandsundry>

Jo-Ann Fabric and Craft Stores
<http://www.youtube.com/user/Joanndotcom>

Make: makezine.com <http://www.youtube.com/user/makemagazine>

Michaels Stores http://www.youtube.com/user/MichaelsStores>

PROJECT WEBSITES

Craftster® <http://www.craftster.org/>

Cut Out +Keep: Make and Share Craft Tutorials
<http://www.cutoutandkeep.net/>

Evil Mad Scientist Laboratories <http://www.evilmadscientist.com/>

MAKE Projects <http://makeprojects/com/>

Upcycle That <http://upcyclethat.com/>

ORGANIZATIONS

20-Time <http://www.20timeineducation.com>
Allowing students time to work independently or collaboratively on a topic of personal interest.

Hackerspaces <hackerspaces.org>
An international community of local Hackerspaces.

Makerspace <makerspace.com>
An online sharing community of makers.

Mentor Makerspace <mentor.makerspace.com>
A make community just for schools and teachers.

SHOPPING

Hobby Lobby® <http://www.hobbylobby.com>
Home Depot® <http://www.homedepot.com>
littleBits <http://shop.littlebits.com>
Maker Shed <http://www.makershed.com>
Michaels® <http://www.michaels.com>
Plug and Wear <http://www.plugandwear.com>
Radio Shack <http://www.radioshack.com>
SheekGeek <http://sheekgeek.com>
Shop at McCall <http://shops.mcccall.com>
SparkFun® Electronics <http://www.sparfun.com>
Velleman® <http://www.vellemanusa.com>

STANDARDS and LEARNING

Common Core: State Standards Initiative. <http://www.corestandards.org/>

"Learning Standards & Program Guidelines", American Library Association, September 12, 2012. <http://www.ala.org/aasl/standards-guidelines> Document ID: 25d01915-3118-a204-c983-9b7aba977255>

"Learning4Life", American Library Association, September 6, 2012. <http://www.ala.org/aasl/learning4life> Document ID: 04376c42-4519-56f4-91e5-74a8553d5320>

Within the makerspace activity, there is a guided exploratory experience to build background knowledge and hands-on experience before working on an independent make. Prior to the doing, students gain understanding through learning from resources, which include books, video, audio, articles, websites, community resources, and mentors. As learning progresses, students take thinking to a deeper level as they involve themselves in more independent makes or work as a team to develop and problem solve more complex projects.

Create

Every makerspace activity is about learning and creating a final product. As young makers gain experiences, they also gain confidence to working independently on more advanced tasks based upon their prior experiences and what they found to be of personal interest.

Utilizing cloud computing, students can work together as both a virtual and face-to-face team to organize their learning and plans. In the school library makerspace community, not only are students sharing knowledge and ideas to create, they are also there to help develop and conceptualize new makerspace activities to be implemented for the future.

Share

Consider the value of being engaged in the global world of makers (see Appendix 4). Some makes require a team to be successful and that group must work together effectively whether it be virtual or as a face-to-face team. Everything in a makerspace is hands-on, real world learning of varying subjects and interests. A makerspace incorporates active participation, development of relationships with others with similar interests, and working collaboratively to create.

As makers' skills develop, they are integral to developing instruction videos, how-to sheets, and pathfinders for future makers or makers new to their expertise. Host a mini-Maker Faire (see Appendix 2). Consider how to make projects that can be used within the community to help those less fortunate, to bring happiness, or to teach others in the community. Contribute successful makes to an online pre-existing make community, or develop an online sharing resource personalized and customized for the school's makerspace.

Grow

A makerspace constructs opportunities for young makers to sample a variety of experiences that are foundational to opening their minds to the endless possibilities for personal growth and independent experiences. Once a student has a basic understanding and some core skills developed, the makerspace is ideal for allowing that student to continue the learning and doing independently. As the makerspace is a volunteer activity and requires reading for understanding and learning, every experience in the makerspace is about personal growth. As students gain knowledge and experience with concepts, they will gain confidence and investigate independently to expand their knowing and doing of a particular make of personal interest. The participants produce something tangible based on what they have learned and done.

Use a school sanctioned web-based communication tool to communicate, collect, and share information; collaborate; and problem-solve. Every makerspace event incorporates the need to create. When a large, or complex, or student-driven make is in progress, interaction among participants is crucial in the learning and making process.

Common Core

College and Career Readiness Anchor Standards for Reading

Integration of Knowledge and Ideas (standards 7, 9) (Common Core State Standards for English Language Arts & Literacy in History/Social Studies, Science, and Technical Subjects 2010)

Any make, but especially an independent challenge, requires participants to learn from a variety of sources to build knowledge. Building understanding as a maker often means learning from experts by reading and seeing, before doing. As makers inquire, it is important for them to recognize conflicting information or discrepancies amongst sources. As the student reads and learns, he may find that there is more than one way to create, or more than one solution, so he will need to analyze the information and work on problem-solving for the best possible solution for himself and his situation.

Range and Reading and Level of Text Complexity (standard 10) (Common Core State Standards for English Language Arts & Literacy in History/Social Studies, Science, and Technical Subjects 2010)

In order for students to learn and grow in a maker environment, it is important to build their knowledge and experience in stages to ensure new, more complicated learning is built upon the foundation of prior learning and experiences. In this way, students can read and comprehend more complex text with new, advanced vocabulary and thinking specific to the task.

College and Career Readiness Anchor Standards for Writing

Text Types and Purposes (standards 2, 4, 6) (Common Core State Standards for English Language Arts & Literacy in History/Social Studies, Science, and Technical Subjects 2010)

Students in a makerspace learn, and as they learn, they create, and as they create, they communicate their knowledge and experiences with others. This is done through informative and explanatory text used to convey the need, purpose, and step-by-step guidance for replication. Writing for this strong purpose requires the writer to produce clear and coherent writing in which the development, organization, and style are appropriate to the task, purpose, and audience.

A makerspace is an ideal place for students to create instructional guides for others to follow and pathfinders of valuable resources which helped her and might help others following in her footsteps. The Internet is ripe with opportunities for students to publish their writing—especially for makers—and collaborate with others of similar interests. See Appendix 2 for ideas for how to get young makers involved in sharing what they learn.

Research to Build and Present Knowledge (standard 8) (Common Core State Standards for English Language Arts & Literacy in History/Social Studies, Science, and Technical Subjects 2010)

While investigating a potential make opportunity, inquiry is key. Students hone research skills with a range of resources, evaluating the integrity and validity of the resources throughout the journey. As the experience progresses, students will need to blend what is learned, building upon that foundation to create new knowledge, yet giving credit to resources, experts, and inspirations in order to avoid plagiarism.

College and Career Readiness Anchor Standards for Speaking and Listening

Comprehension and Collaboration (standard 1) (Common Core State Standards for English Language Arts & Literacy in History/Social Studies, Science, and Technical Subjects 2010)

Through group makerspace projects, communication is essential. Students work together with others in groups. They could possibly call on an expert mentor either in person or virtually, and work within a cloud environment to communicate, share, and problem solve with others in their group, or other groups working on the same project but in a different time, or even place.

Presentation of Knowledge and Ideas (standards 4, 5) (Common Core State Standards for English Language Arts & Literacy in History/Social Studies, Science, and Technical Subjects 2010)

Makers relate information through presentations within the local maker community. They create how-to visual guides to share on the web, step-by-step instructions for the school library makerspace, instructional videos, and presentations for events like a mini-Maker Faire. Through these complex communication tasks, students are learning how to communicate effectively.

Mathematics: Standards for Mathematical Practice

(standards 1, 3, 4, 6) (Common Core Standards for Mathematics 2010)

When working with a technical make, like when utilizing an Arduino, or a spatial make, like designing a swing set for a local community center, working individually or as a team to accurately calculate the mathematical issues is integral to the success of the make. When working within a maker team to construct a complicated make, it is often necessary to check others' work to ensure accuracy. Conversely, it is also important to be able to argue and defend when a student thinks their mathematical solution is justified. Mathematics will often be needed to solve simple spatial or more complex, electronic problems within the context of the make. Students will need to take what they know about math and apply it to solve problems or find solutions within the make. Integral to a makerspace is sharing make experiences, problems, solutions, and how others could replicate a success. In order for others to successfully recreate a project, the maker must be precise in instructions, including communicating accurate mathematical formulas and measurements.

STEM: Science, Technology, Engineering, and Math

STEM (Science, Technology, Engineering, and Math) skills are integral to thinking and doing in this exponentially expanding information, techno-gadget overloaded, thinking-and-doing society. It is imperative that education and educators foster STEM learning and a school library makerspace is an ideal place to encourage STEM exploration in a fun, productive, club-like, friendly environment. Further explore STEM ideas in Appendices 2, 3, and 4.

Communication

In a school library makerspace, there is thinking and learning and doing. But there is also storytelling. There is a need to communicate what was done and share with others the experience as well as how to repeat the process. Teaching is a craft and although everyone can learn and do at some level, not everyone has the opportunity to expand the depth of that learning through teaching. To teach is to truly know a subject and it is an important part of the learning process to be able to impart knowledge in a manner in which others can understand. Share with the school community about why it was done, how it was done, and how to replicate the process. This can be done through displays or live informal or formal presentations. Communication can be digital postings in a cloud or public posting to reputable websites which include recorded video, audio, images, illustrations, written text, or a combination thereof. Not only does this assist the library's maker community by adding to their pool of knowledge, it also assists the maker by expanding their ability to communicate and think through the learning and doing in a more finite, systematic manner. See Appendix 2 and 4 for organization and communication ideas.

Mentors

The word mentor has a deep history, dating back to Homer's *Odyssey*. In *The Odyssey*, Mentor is the advisor of young Telemachus. When Odysseus goes off to war, he leaves the care of his son, Telemachus, to Mentor (Homer). Mentor has come to mean a wise and trusted friend, advisor, and teacher ("Mentor" 2006). Mentors are important and necessary components to advanced, complex, and independent makerspace projects (Makerspace Team 2012). School librarians match the self-selected project task and young person or group to an expert in the field. This is a maker mentor. Maker mentors could be found through local trade unions, tech companies, universities, craft and hobby societies, and makerspace support sites (see Appendix 4). For example, could young makers gain valuable experience and understanding through collaborating with a local computer programmer before initiating an Arduino?

When sanctioning a mentorship, be sure to follow school district safety policies, procedures, and permissions already in place for volunteers, coaches, and artists-in-residence. It is important for the safety of students that all appropriate precautions are taken to ensure their emotional, intellectual, and physical welfare when sponsoring an in-person or virtual guest expert.

Safety, Rules, and Instructions

Establish clearly defined general rules and makerspace policy. These should include safety, clean-up procedures, and the sacredness of others' projects. Be prepared to follow-up with appropriate consequences for breaches of agreement to makerspace policies. As well as the general rules and makerspace policy, each make will also have precautions specific to the task.

Safety

Be sure to clearly state the safety rules and requirements in the school library makerspace. Ensure that the makerspace complies with all local and state safety procedures and requirements. Always consider that any activity should be treated with respect and care. For each activity, consider the safety precautions necessary for students and the inherent risks involved. Even the most innocuous task has inherent risk. Research the subject and work through the activity, thinking like a young maker and patron to better anticipate potential gaffes. An activity which may be appropriate for one group or age level may not be the right fit for another group or age level. For every activity, consult the local, do-it-yourself hardware store, or expert in the related field for the essential precautions and safety gear necessary.

Consult with school administration. Do students and/or parents need to sign a permission or release for students to use certain tools? Should participants sign a safety contract for the year? Should parents or guardians sign a permission slip before students may participate in certain projects?

Rules

Institute rules for respecting others' work. Many projects will require multiple visits, so create a system for storing, saving, and protecting projects in progress. Projects will sometimes require return visits, either due to time constraints or the nature of the project. For example, something may require drying before moving on to the next step. Or a self-directed project will take more time due to the complexity of the task for researching, planning, designing, and then constructing. Other times, projects will be collaborative in nature, so a clear understanding must be enforced for a group consensus on moving the project forward without destroying the previous efforts of the group.

Instructions

It is important to test and make a sample of any building knowledge and experiences-level activity. This is for modeling and display purposes, but is also important because only by creating one in advance, will it be clear if there are supplies missing, safety issues, or inconsistencies in training, learning, or instructional means. This is also a chance to realize if it is possible to substitute a supply item for something already on hand, a more affordable alternate, or a better fit for your situation or patrons. By creating a sample, it also gives the librarian a more clear idea of whether it is an activity truly appropriate for the learning objective and the patron's abilities. Going through the process also provides a better vision for any safety issues and precautions necessary.

Badges, Merit Patches, Participation Recognition

It is human nature to feel intrinsically good about successes. There is a sense of self-satisfaction in fulfilling a task and seeing the accomplishment of a final product. School libraries are promoters of lifelong learning and self-edification. A library's collection, both digital and print, and environmental, are to support the quest for independent thought and lifelong learning. Those successes can also be measured with a small, yet significant and symbolic, extrinsic marker of learning and success. Look at the tradition of the Boy Scouts of America®, the Girls Scouts of the United States of America, and 4-H for their popular means of recognizing young people successfully completing the learning required to accomplish a task. They reward with patches and ribbons. These tokens are often developed into a collection to be ogled with pride. Consider ways in which a local school library makerspace might give a small token of personal recognition. These could be earned from novice to emerging to independent for learning, leveling up to greater degrees of difficult and complexity related to the specific make theme, like soft circuitry. This could be a ribbon, badge, pin, sticker, or stamp for each makerspace skill achieved or project completed.

Digital Badges

The recognition of skills, experiences, learning, or tasks completed could also be electronic, yet still tangible with virtual badges earned and collected. Consider USA Swimming and the Deck Pass app. With this app, swimmers work to earn hundreds of e-patches through attending meets, participating in other sanctioned functions, and reaching certain goals and speeds in particular events. Like the patches that used to be hand-sewn onto warm-up suits, young swimmers now collect patches electronically and save them on an electronic device.

In 2011, the US Department of Education shared the notion of digital badges, a concept which could be adapted for library makerspaces (Duncan September 15, 2011). Digital badges could be collected, stored, and shared in an eco-friendly, electronic platform. Digital badges would be earned as a measure of a certain makerspace skill achieved, collected in what is called a backpack, and shared through social media. Consider Mozilla's Open Badges: http://open badges.org, badg.us: http://badg.us, ClassBadges: http://classbadges.com, or edmodo's badges: http://help.edmodo.com/teachers/how-to-createmanage-badges/. A classic model for digital maker badges, which look strikingly similar to traditional Girl Scout badges, are DIY's skills patches (see Appendix 4). For further reading about digital badges, check out the annotated bibliography provided by HASTAC (Humanities, Arts, Science and Technology Advanced Collaboratory), *Digital Badges: An Annotated Research Bibliography v1* (http://hastac.org/digital-badges-bibliography).

Supplies

Begin collecting random items others might consider scraps or junk, but could be future project treasures. Repurposing, reusing, or recycling will help students learn to be eco-friendly and save on makerspace expenses. Storing collections of supplies will allow the creators of school library makerspaces to be ready for many random, yet valuable, ideas which are inspired, spontaneous mash-ups of a conglomeration of ideas. Commandeer community volunteers to help build the foundational store of supplies: PTA/PTO organizations, staff, students, community outreach, and recycle facilities.

Look for great seasonal, beginning of the school year deals for project staples to stock and save.

- Cleaning supplies
- Disposable gloves
- Erasers
- Folders

- Glue and glue sticks
- Crayons, markers, pencils, pens, colored pencils
- Medical supplies
- Paper: lined, graph, copy
- Resealable plastic baggies
- Rulers
- Scissors
- Containers for projects in progress and storing supplies

Begin immediately accumulating a core collection of materials. These are items which inspire and are easily adapted to DIY maker activities. The supplies needed vary, depending on the makerspace focus, but a few ideas to consider include:

- Balsa wood and wood scraps
- Beads and buttons
- Card stock and colored paper
- Circuit board kits: Arduino, littleBits, Velleman® (see Appendix 3)
- Fabric, felt
- Glues: wood, craft, super, fabric
- Newsprint or butcher paper (an inexpensive write-on planning spaces and workspace mat)
- Nuts and bolts
- Sandpaper
- Stickers and foam shapes
- Tapes: paper, crafting, duct tape, painters, masking
- Yarn, cording, ribbon, thread

People often get interested in a craft or hobby, only to go on to something new. What to do with all those no longer needed materials? Let co-workers, friends, neighbors, PTA, and family know that you will accept anything they no longer use. Build a reputation for accepting even the craziest items, because sometimes unique and eclectic is inspirational for the young maker or the program coordinator's next project.

Plan ahead and begin posting a request for donations in the student newsletter and on the school website months, or even a year, in advance of when those supplies will be needed. If there is a local community or student newspaper, those also might run a monthly or quarterly makerspace donation request for free.

Contact local recycling centers to see if there are "shopping" days for educators. The recycle center is a good place to collect a sundry of odd, but usable makerspace items for upcycling projects: keyboard keys, puzzle pieces, seasonal and party decorations, office supplies, school supplies, craft supplies, vinyl records, game pieces, plastics, cardboard, laminate tiles, and

Mustang Makerspace Donations Needed

The school library Mustang Makerspace is seeking donations to help with student projects. If you have any of the following items to donate, please deliver them to Mrs. Preddy, School Librarian, in the Library Media Center.

- Used Gift Cards
- Old Men's Ties
- Resealable Plastic Bags (all sizes)
- Old Picture Frames (5x7 or 8x10)
- Hardware
  (nuts, bolts, washers, screws)
- Empty Glass Jars (lids not needed)
- Buttons
- Super Glue®
- Wax paper and Aluminum Foil
- Fabric Scraps
- Scrapbooking Paper Scraps

Thank you for your help.

various assortments of craft and hand tools. If there is something specific needed, the recycle center may be able to keep a lookout for what is needed and set it aside for pickup. For example, when I needed computer keyboard keys for an activity, I called the local recycle agency and within two days, I was called to the facility to pick keys off keyboards, walking out with pounds of the needed keys.

Recycling is a makerspace budget lifesaver. With a little cleaning and some prep work, many different project ideas can utilize the following recycled items:

- Books weeded from the collection or salvaged from the recycling bin
- Cardboard
- Countertop tile samples and chips
- Egg cartons, which are good for holding paint and other liquids, or organizing small objects
- Gift wrap and tissue paper
- Glass jars (with and without lids)
- Greeting cards
- Magazines and catalogs
- Milk cartons: individual, gallon, half gallon
- Paint sample strip
- Plastic gift cards
- Plastic take-away containers and food canisters (these can be used for projects as well as storing supplies)
- Puzzle pieces
- Small metal tins with lids (like Altoids containers)
- Wallpaper and upholstery books
- Wood scraps

Equipment can be quite costly to purchase and maintain, so think carefully, do the due diligence to research the best fit, and only purchase what will be used and can be maintained. Also consider the cost of supplies. For example, only purchase a 3D printer if the cost of the supplies to make prototypes fits into the annual makerspace budget. Depending on the age, project, supervision levels, and cost, consider the makerspace equipment needs, which might include:

- 3D printer
- Book press (if you already have one)
- Clamps and vices
- Computer peripherals: color printer, scanner
- Computers with Internet access
- Crafting Punches
- Cutting mats
- Digital cameras for still and video
- Glue guns
- Hand tools: crimping tools, files, hammer, mallet, pliers, punches, screwdrivers, utility knife and cutters, wrenches, level
- Iron and tabletop iron pad
- Microwave
- Microwave flower press
- Miter box and miter saw

- Paper trimmer with cutting blades and scoring blade attachment
- Safety goggles, gloves, aprons
- Scissors: craft, decorative edge, sewing, industrial
- Sewing machine (inexpensive for simple straight stitch and zigzag)
- Sewing needles, pins, safety pins
- Slow cookers of varying sizes
- Soldering iron
- Tacking iron
- Tape measure
- Toaster oven
- Warming plate

References

American Library Association. "AASL Standards for the 21st-Century Learner." Last modified November 08, 2006. Accessed February 17, 2013. http://www.ala.org/aasl/standards-guidelines/learning-standards. Document ID: ec710ea2-99a2-27d4-b987-e042c9f4bf3f.

Anderson, Chris. *Makers. The New Industrial Revolution.* New York: Crown Business, 2012.

Duncan, Arne. U.S. Department of Education, "Digital Badges for Learning: Remarks by Secretary Duncan at 4th Annual Launch of the MacArthur Foundation Digital Media and Lifelong Learning Competition." Last modified September 15, 2011. Accessed January 4, 2013. http://www.ed.gov/news/speeches/digital-badges-learning.

Homer. *The Odyssey.* Project Gutenberg, 2002. eBook.

Makerspace Team. "Makerspace Playbook DRAFT." *makerspace.com.* April 2012. http://makerspacedotcom.files.wordpress.com/2012/04/makerspaceplaybook-201204.pdf.

Merriam-Webster's Dictionary and Thesaurus. Springfield: Merriam-Webster, Incorporated, 2006. s.v. "Mentor."

National Governors Association Center for Best Practices, Council of Chief State School Officers, "Common Core State Standards for English Language Arts & Literacy in History/Social Studies, Science, and Technical Subjects." 2010. Accessed January 20, 2013. http://www.corestandards.org/assets/CCSSI_ELA Standards.pdf.

National Governors Association Center for Best Practices, Council of Chief State School Officers, "Common Core Standards for Mathematics." Last modified 2010. Accessed January 20, 2013. http://www.corestandards.org/assets/CCSSI_Math Standards.pdf.

Library Makerspace Programming and Activities

Select activities for the makerspace meet creativity goals for new learning and academic standards, with a dose of technical and dexterity skills included. There are a range of student interests, abilities, and prior knowledge, as well as a plethora of experiences students can't even imagine because they don't even know of their existence or the possibilities available to young people. Develop a breadth and scope of activities which cover a variety of fine arts, crafts, sciences, hobbies, technology, and twenty-first century technical skills. Activities can be group construction, individual, or simple make-n-take. It might be something done in one sitting, or requires several return trips, or even weeks to complete. A group activity could be creating a giant tetrahedron, constructing a tent-size igloo out of milk cartons, stitching together a patchwork quilt, no-bake cooking for a community fundraiser, or working creatively with various types of puzzles, magnetic poetry, or Legos. Individual goals and foundational experiences could be bookmarks, jewelry, book covers, pressed flowers, greeting cards, foldables, seasonal ideas, and repurposed/recycled inspirations. Technology could be circuitry, Lego® Digital Design, video production, fabrication, or app invention. Further ideas and inspiration are located in Appendix 3.

Keep connected to various educational and community organizations in order to keep well-informed of local and national opportunities. These offer free promotion and implementation documents; some of which might provide free supplies as well. Most require registration through an email request or web-based registration form to unlock the programming resources or to be placed on the mailing list to receive the gratis event materials. Some event opportunities may require a little tweaking to fit the ability or age level of your patrons. See Appendix 2 for a quick-start list of organizations and events.

Creative Commons

As makers are encouraged to give credit to their project inspirations, makers also need to learn how to maintain credits and rights to their intellectual property, ensuring they also receive credit for their creative efforts. This can be a simple, free process through attaining a Creative Commons (CC) license. A CC allows the maker to decide how their music, video, code, text, and art may be shared and distributed. Students can use the license-choosing tool to decide which of the six licenses is the best fit: http://creativecommons.org/choose/. Currently, CC does not charge a fee for licensing.

Makerspace Projects

A makerspace task can revolve around the creation of anything imagined. Initially, it might be easier to use all tried-and-true activities already tested for successful application and use them exactly as created and prescribed. For example, search Appendix 3 for inspiring ideas which others have not only successfully completed, but in the vein of the maker community, shared. Or an idea, maybe something you thought of, a memory you have from childhood activities, something shared by somebody else, a 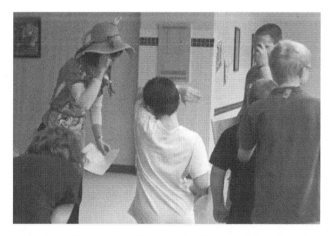 workshop or conference experience, seeing something else out and about in the world to inspire a concept, or the idea was found within a periodical, book, or the Internet. The muse for an activity may come from a lesson plan, holiday, commercial, professional conversation, event in a fictional read, visit to a place, movie or television or webisode, or any number of other random, everyday experiences. Once looking at things from a different perspective, inspiration will be found around every corner. Teach yourself and your young makers to begin viewing the world for inspirational possibilities. A makerspace project could be an amalgamation. For example, when I went to the local community recycle center to shop, there was a box of laminate tile samples. I had seen these tiles used in the elementary school as library identification cards, but also in the back of my mind was my concern about the local family shelter. The kids have so little to play with when they enter the shelter, but what they do have must be small and portable. Then I thought about my daughter's lifelong love of memory games. So, what if students were challenged to design custom memory games out of laminate chips to donate to children in the local shelter? What might be needed to accomplish the project? How would students decide themes and plan their designs? How could the artwork be constructed and what supplies would be needed? Who should we contact to partner with a family shelter to ensure the games made it into the hands of children in need?

Consider these suggestions for further and engaging inspiration:

- Investigate the school and local library's collection for books and periodicals on fine arts, crafts, hobbies, science fair projects, games, technology activities, and other hands-on skills and inspirations.
- Attend conferences, workshops, and technology and craft fairs.
- Frequent home improvement, hobby, and craft stores and their companion websites for idea stimulation. See Appendix 3 for suggestions.
- Subscribe to electronic newsletters which spotlight potential ideas and makerspace projects. To get started, some newsletter subscription links are listed in Appendix 3 and Appendix 4.
- Attend the 4-H exhibits at the county fair and other local and regional events which exhibit young people's ingenuity and creativity in action. Be inspired and amazed by all which can be seen.

Community

Purposeful learning, community service, service learning, civic responsibility—a makerspace may sometimes be about meaningful doing. A community has needs. A school has needs. Sometimes these necessities or wants cannot be done through traditional budgets and avenues. This is where the makerspace can make a difference and have a constructive and positive impact on the community. There could be a purpose to the work based on community or school needs, whether it be making life better through humanitarian efforts or aesthetic improvements. The work effort and creativity of students could be used productively to make a difference within the school or community. This could be creating learning materials to meet the needs of other students, this could be helping a community organization or nonprofit, this could be a beautification project for the community, or this could be hosting a workshop to teach others how to do a make.

When partnering to donate makes to people in a community place, attach a small card to each object explaining its origin and have the maker write a personal note on the back to the receiver.

> This was made especially for you
> by a participant of the
> Perry Meridian Middle School
> Mustang Makers.
>
> This club was made possible through a grant
> from Perry Township Education Foundation.

THINK: LEARNING AND BUILDING KNOWLEDGE

- The Foundation for a Better Life. http://www.values.com
- Global Youth Service Day. http://www.gysd.org
- Pay it Forward Foundation. http://www.payitforwardfoundation.org
- Random Acts of Kindness Foundation. http://www.randomactsofkindness.org
- United States Environmental Protection Agency. "Community Service." http://www.epa.gov/students/communityservice.html
- Volunteer.gov "Natural and Cultural Resources Volunteer Portal." http://www.volunteer.gov/Gov/
- Youth Service America. http://www.ysa.org/

DIY: Do It Yourself

DIY stands for Do It Yourself. It is about making, transforming, or repairing an object or place. Traditionally, it has meant something in the home. Recently, that definition has expanded to mean any getting-your-hands-dirty opportunity to make, create, or produce something constructive. Rather than buying it or paying for someone else to do it, learning to use the tools and supplies, and building the skills necessary to do it for yourself. The learning is grass-roots with official, professional training limited to workshops, readings, video, and trial and error practice.

THINK: LEARNING AND BUILDING KNOWLEDGE

- Craftster®. http://www.craftster.org
- The DIY Club. http://thediyclub.com
- DIY Guides. "DIY Clubs." https://diy.org/guides/clubs
- DIY Network. http://www.diynetwork.com
- Fixers. "A Film About Repair." http://ifixit.org/fixers-film
- iFixit. "Self Repair Manifesto." http://www.ifixit.com/Manifesto
- PBS Newshour. "Can DIY Movement Fix a Crisis in U.S. Science Education?" (video) http://www.pbs.org/newshour/bb/science/jan-june11/makerfaire_06 -29.html
- *Reader's Digest Complete Do-It-Yourself Manual: Completely Revised and Updated.* Reader's Digest, 2005.

Foodcrafting and Food Gardens

The makerspace is an ideal place to experiment, study, explore, and creatively interact with foods, food preparation, spices, nutrition, and herb and vegetable gardening. It has been a national trend to remove food preparation, nutrition, and family and consumer science programs from the schools. Due in part to that situation, we have generations of students growing up with little or no experience cooking, baking, caring for their nutritional future, or preparing and implementing meal menus. Today's television, apps, books, and Internet allow for many opportunities to view recipes and cooking shows in order to learn from experts and to see how to experiment with recipes by mixing various ingredients and measurements to alter the outcome. Microwaves, toaster ovens, and slow cookers allow for experimenting and expedient cooking. Opportunities to experiment by altering recipes for single serving, updating recipes to include modern conveniences, and testing out new concoctions is a makerspace fit. For example, I have been hosting a makerspace cooking club and all year we have been working on basic preparation skills, nutrition, following instructions, and recipes requiring simple, inexpensive ingredients that students can easily and affordably replicate at home. This has been so successful, the kids have had so much growth and gained so much confidence in the kitchen, they have requested our last meeting be a pitch-in so they can each make and share something that they made, a recipe they found and steps they followed on their own, as an individual. It is important for young people today to understand that they can eat well even if they don't have a lot of money. They also don't want to take a lot of time in the making, so they need to learn to make healthy, quick meals.

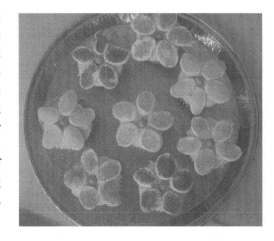

THINK: LEARNING AND BUILDING KNOWLEDGE

- allrecipes.com®. http://allrecipes.com
- *Better Homes and Gardens New Cook Book: Gifts from the Kitchen.* Meredith Corporation, 2012.
- Cooks.com: Cooking, Recipes and More. http://www.cooks.com
- Epic Reads. "YA Inspired Recipes." (blog) http://www.epicreads.com/blog/ya -inspired-recipes

- Food.com™: Home of the Home Cook. "Microwave Recipes." http://www.food.com/recipes/microwave/quickandeasy
- Growing Greener World with Joe Gardener®. "Episodes." (videos) http://www.growingagreenerworld.com/episodes/#
- Infoplease. "Cooking Weights and Measures." http://www.infoplease.com/ipa /A0001723.html
- National Garden Association. http://www.garden.org
- United States Department of Agriculture. "ChooseMyPlate." http://www.choosemyplate.gov
- United States Department of Agriculture. "Nutrition.gov." http://www.nutrition .gov
- United States Department of Agriculture. "Recipe Finder." http://recipefinder .nal.usda.gov
- Vinton, Sherri Brooks. *Put 'em Up!: A Comprehensive Home Preserving Guide for the Creative Cook from Drying and Freezing to Canning and Pickling.* Story Publishing, 2010.

Fashion and Textiles

Couture has been quite a trend in the DIY movement with the freeform sewing method, which does not require a traditional pattern. So now there are new progressive ways to pattern, cut, sew, and incorporate electronics into textiles. Whether male or female, fashion can be very personal and young people can show their independence of personality and strength of character through their fashion sense. Fabric comes from a range of materials including the natural, synthetic, and recycled. Students can learn to use these new and traditional textiles with modern tools, simple sewing machines, a little bit of creativity, trial and error experimentation, and even electronics to add lights, sounds, and other interactiveness to fashion.

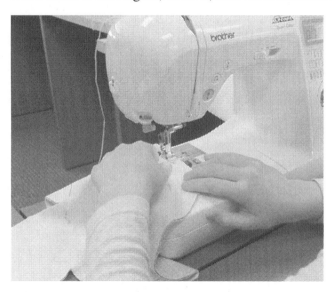 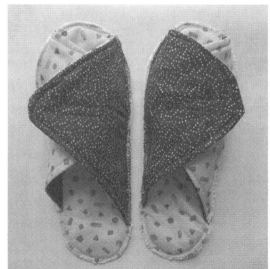

THINK: LEARNING AND BUILDING KNOWLEDGE

- ABC News Video. "Carrie Underwood Grammy Dress: Designer Reveals Secrets." (video) http://abcnews.go.com/GMA/video/grammys-2013-carrie -underwood-dress-designer-don-oneill-18475201
- Blum, Nicole and Debra Immerqut. *Improv Sewing: A Freeform Approach to Creative Techniques; 101 Fast, Fun, and Fearless Projects: Dresses, Tunics, Scarves, Skirts, Accessories, Pillows, Curtains, and More.* Storey Publishing, 2012.
- CuteCircuit. http://cutecircuit.com
- DIYcouture. http://www.diy-couture.co.uk/home.html
- Martin, Rosie. *DIY Couture: Create Your Own Fashion Collection.* Laurence King Publishers. 2012.
- Pakhchyan, Syuzi. *Fashioning Technology: A DIY Intro to Smart Crafting.* O'Reilly Media 2008.
- sewbox.co.uk™. "DIY Couture." http://www.sewbox.co.uk/sewing-patterns/diy -couture.html
- Singer. "Operation Basics." http://www.singerco.com/sewing-resources /operation-basics
- Soft Circuit Saturdays. http://softcircuitsaturdays.com
- Talktomyshirt. "Everything You Want to Know About Wearable Electronics." (blog) http://www.talk2myshirt.com/blog/
- Trash to Couture. (blog) http://www.trashtocouture.com/p/diy.html

Fine Arts

Fine arts are appreciated for their aesthetics, without a high level of practical function. Included might be painting, sculpture, drawing, mixed media, and, for our purposes, also music, drama, poetry, dance, and creative writing. Uninspired, unsure, or intimidated by the fine arts concept? Tour the local museum of art, visit the local community arts center, speak to art instructors, watch a community theatre production, and attend adult how-to art workshops. Attend a beginner's workshop or have fun with friends at an adult make-and-take event, like a dinner and art evening or a Wine and Canvas: www.wineandcanvas.com. Consult with a local artist to be a maker mentor. Let students experiment and contribute inspirations.

THINK: LEARNING AND BUILDING KNOWLEDGE

- Art is Fun! http://www.art-is-fun.com
- ArtRage. http://www.artrage.com/artrage-4.html
- *Color Matters.* "Basic Color Theory." http://www.colormatters.com/color-and -design/basic-color-theory
- *Color Matters.* Color Voodoo®. (eBook PDF) http://www.colorvoodoo.com /colormatters.html
- Fine Art. "Fine Art – Definition & Meaning." http://www.visual-arts-cork.com /definitions/fine-art.htm
- Notation Software™. "Music Notation Software for Everyday Musicians." http:// www.notation.com/NotationComposer.php
- Sax® School Specialty®. http://store.schoolspecialty.com
- The Scribbles Institute™. "Videos." http://scribblesinstitute.com/sample -page-2/

Hobbies and Crafts Revised

Hobbies and crafts include, but are not limited to, basket weaving, beekeeping, body care products, candles, card making, cartooning, ceramics and pottery, crochet, flower arranging, flower pressing, jewelry making, knitting, leathercrafts, macramé, metalwork, paper cutting, paper folding, papier mâché, photography, rubber stamping, scrapbooking, sewing, stained glass, stenciling, weaving, and woodworking. Each has its own proficiencies with a learning curve which requires time, patience, and practice to scaffold abilities from a strong basic skills foundation.

There are many traditional crafts, like leathercraft and woodworking, which require many higher-level thinking skills but also require a financial investment or time investment which may not be feasible in some school settings. Instead, these hobbies can be adapted to today's situation so that the higher-level thinking skills are still there, the originality of the craft which inspired still exists, and yet it's become doable and feasible. Knitting on a knitting loom can be done in half the time required to teach traditional knitting, but the looms are more costly than traditional knitting needles. Reduce expenses by making and practicing on a simple loom made with a paint stir stick, popsicle sticks, duct tape, and some yarn instead of an investment of a store-bought knitting loom for every

participant. In this way, students still get the experience. They get the outcome. They get the thinking necessary to complete a complicated task. Yet it can be done in less time, less money, and with more accessible resources.

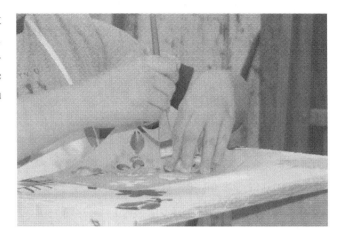

THINK: LEARNING AND BUILDING KNOWLEDGE

- Adamson, Glenn. *The Craft Reader*. Berg Publishers, 2010.
- The Crafty PC™. http://www.thecraftypc.com/index.html
- Favecraft. "Free Craft eBooks." http://www.favecrafts.com/index.php/hct /Free-Craft-eBooks
- Interweave™ Store. http://www.interweavestore.com
- Lion Brand® Yarns. Learning Center. http://www.lionbrand.com/cgi-bin/pg.cgi ?page=learningCenter.html
- The Mountain Laurel. "Arts and Crafts." http://www.mtnlaurel.com/arts-and -crafts.html
- Prime Publishing. "favecrafts." http://www.favecrafts.com
- Sewing.org. "SEW-lutions Guidelines" http://www.sewing.org/html/guidelines .html
- YouCanMakeThis.com. http://www.youcanmakethis.com/index.htm

STEM: Science, Technology, Engineering, and Math

STEM stands for science, technology, engineering, and math. STEM are often key to standards and skills in makerspace activities. STEM fosters learning opportunities, resources, and career awareness in the school through instruction, inquiry, and applied learning opportunities. Key skills to the STEM learning and teaching concept are building curiosity, creativity, collaboration, communication, and critical thinking skills. It is helping students maintain their inquisitive nature as they question and process the world around them in order to be innovative and provoke thought. The makerspace will be especially important in coming years with the focus on STEM in schools and meeting the national desire to interest women and minorities toward

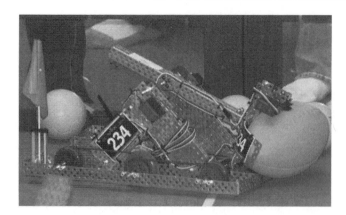

STEM career paths. School library makerspaces are integral to meeting STEM goals of curiosity, creativity, collaboration, communication, inquiry, and critical thinking skills.

THINK: LEARNING AND BUILDING KNOWLEDGE

- Andrade, Pedro Nakazato. "Recovering Mobility After A Bone Fracture." http://www.pedroandrade.com/Bones-is-an-orthopedic-cast-with-sensors-for-capturing-muscle
- Banzi, Massimo. *Getting Started with Arduino*. Make. 2011.
- Discovery Education. "Connect the Dots: STEM CAMP." http://www.discoveryeducation.com/STEM
- First Book® STEM Science, Technology, Engineering and Math. "Resources." http://stem.firstbook.org/resources
- Lifehacker. "Tips, Tricks, and Downloads for Getting Things Done." http://lifehacker.com
- NASA. "Space Technology Mission Directorate." http://www.nasa.gov/directorates/spacetech/home/index.html
- National Lab Network. http://www.nationallabnetwork.org
- NSTA: "STEM Forum and Expo Annual Conference." http://www.nsta.org/conferences
- PBS Teachers. "STEM Education Resource Center" http://www.pbs.org/teachers/stem
- STEMconnector®. "The One Stop Shop for Stem Information." http://www.stemconnector.org
- Sousa, David A. and Thomas J. Pilecki. *From STEM to STEAM: Using Brain-Compatible Strategies to Integrate the Arts*. Corwin. 2013.

Teamwork

Teamwork is often required throughout life and work. It is a skill set which is hard to teach, hard to learn, and can only be built through repetitive practice and experience. A strength in any individual is their ability to work with a group to problem solve, create, think, follow through, get along, sometimes lead and sometimes follow, and enjoy the doing within a group.

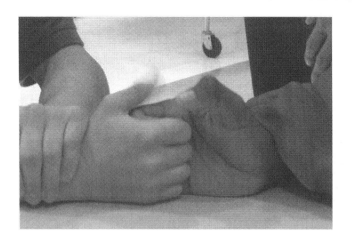

THINK: LEARNING AND BUILDING KNOWLEDGE

- Atherton, J. S. Teaching and Learning. "Using the Class Group: Group Development." http://www.learningandteaching.info/teaching/group_development.htm
- Burdett, Jane and Brianne Hastie. "Predicting Satisfaction with Group Work Assignments." *Journal of University Teaching & Learning Practice*, 2009. (ERIC EJ867297) http://www.eric.ed.gov/PDFS/EJ867297.pdf
- Frey, Nancy, Douglas Fisher, and Sandi Everlove. *Productive Group Work: How to Engage Students, Build Teamwork, and Promote Understanding*. Association for Supervision & Curriculum Development, 2009.
- Project-Management-Skills.com. "Teamwork In The Workplace." http://www.project-management-skills.com/teamwork-in-the-workplace.html
- Smith, Mark K. "Kurt Lewin: groups, experiential learning and action research." http://www.infed.org/thinkers/et-lewin.htm

Repurposing Books and Periodicals

One item the school library has an abundance of are annually weeded books and periodicals. There are often professional discussions about what to do with these books. There is a level of guilt in throwing them out, but if not good enough for the library, how could they be good for anyone? They could be utilized in the school library makerspaces to repurpose, recycle, and upcycle. Instead of throwing these out or putting them in the recycle bin, think about how to use bits and  pieces. Repurpose in various manners to create new and useful materials or pieces of art. Or keep the book whole, but change it into an art form called altered books. As an altered book, the book shape remains, but is converted into a different type of book, a piece of art, a journal, storage container, or other vision imagined by the creator.

THINK: LEARNING AND BUILDING KNOWLEDGE

- *Altered Books.* (series) Design Originals Publishing, copyright varies.
- altered.book.com. "Arts and Craft Definitions." http://www.altered-book.com /arts-and-craft.html
- American Library Association. "Weeding Library Collections: A Selected Annotated Bibliography for Library Collection Evaluation." http://www.ala.org /tools/libfactsheets/alalibraryfactsheet15
- Dishfunctional Designs. "Bookish-Upcycled & Repurposed Books and Pages." (blog) http://dishfunctionaldesigns.blogspot.com/2011/12/artfrom-pages-of -book.html
- Leigh, Elizah. "Read Between the Lines of Old Books with These Repurposing Ideas." Reuse. http://1800recycling.com/2011/08/read-between-lines-recycling -books-repurposing-ideas
- The Paper Mill Store. "Paper Making." (video) https://www.youtube.com /watch?v=7SdJtYkAzTw
- Thompson, Jason. *Playing with Books: The Art of Upcycling, Deconstructing, and Reimagining the Book.* Quarry Books, 2010.

Upcycling Crafts

Upcycling is taking something that is no longer needed in its original form or for its original purpose and repurposing it for a new need or into a new form. This is a great way for students to actively learn how to reduce their carbon footprint. By thinking differently about things around homes and throughout the community, they could look at the world in a different way and create new and useful purposes for pre-existing materials. Upcycling is the reuse component of reduce, reuse, recycle by taking materials that would've been thrown away or tossed aside and finding an effective purpose for them.

The supplies for upcycling crafts may be collected year-round as the original need is done, and a new purpose has yet to be resolved or discovered. There doesn't have to be an immediate need for it; just keep an open mind and vision, collecting materials as they become available for future possibility. It is amazing how many times supplies are needed and I am able to go back to my magic cabinets and find exactly what we need for a sudden inspiration that a student has for a make. To be able to come up with supplies, at immediate need, has a strong impact on a young makers enthusiasm and attitude.

THINK: LEARNING AND BUILDING KNOWLEDGE

- Craftbits.com. "Recycled Crafts." http://www.craftbits.com/recycled-crafts
- Craftideas.info. "Recycling Crafts." http://www.craftideas.info/html/recycling_crafts_b.html
- ECO-foryou.com. "Even the Chaos Has Some Order." http://www.eco-foryou.com/
- Hipcycle Presents. "What is Upcycling?" (video) http://vimeopro.com/hipcycle/the-hipcycle-channel/video/28180203
- House, Allan. *Big Green Book of Recycled Crafts.* Leisure Arts, 2009.
- Make-Stuff. "Recycling." http://www.make-stuff.com/indexes/recyclingindex.html
- Missouri Department of Natural Resources. "Solid Waste Management Program." http://www.dnr.mo.gov/env/swmp/pubs-reports/threers.htm
- National Institute of Environmental Health Sciences. "Quotations on the Environment and Nature." http://kids.niehs.nih.gov/explore/ehs/qtnature.htm
- National Wildlife Federation. "Salvaging and Reusing Wood" http://www.nwf.org/How-to-Help/Live-Green/Reduce-Reuse-Recycle/Wood.aspx
- "Reuse It Or Lose It." New York State Department of Environmental Conservation. (booklet) http://www.dec.ny.gov/docs/materials_minerals_pdf/reusit.pdf
- United States Environmental Protection Agency. "Reduce, Reuse, Recycle." http://www.epa.gov/recycle
- United States Environmental Protection Agency. "Wastes-Resource Conservation-Common Waste & Materials." http://www.epa.gov/osw/conserve/materials

---

Activities

The following school makerspace activities are of varying subjects, complexity, and expense to give a kick start to your school makerspace. Included are hands-on experiences which guide the makerspace coordinator toward developing novice through advanced programming for each concept. When reviewing these activities, follow the model for the school library makerspace projects to advance in stages from learning and building knowledge, an introductory hands-on activity through a guided task, to growing through completing a challenge without step-by-step, to sharing with others. Finally, not included, but implied in every makerspace event, is a self-selected and fully independent objective. When setting up for a makerspace activity, be sure to review Chapter 1 for start-up advice.

Introduction

Each activity begins with an introduction. The introduction explains the idea's inspiration and a basic explanation of the topic. Read the introduction to gain a general understanding as well as an example for how to look at the world for makerspace project ideas from everyday conversations, experiences, and moments.

Think

Books, videos, blogs, websites, and other resources are provided to provide a foundation. Select from the resources provided, or research to add or update selections, for makers to engage in and build a foundation of knowledge before beginning the make.

Create

Students need basic, hands-on, make experience with guidance, direction, and training before they can begin working independently. This section of each activity offers step-by-step instruction as well as a list of suggested equipment, supplies, and optional materials necessary. The guided instruction includes demonstrative pictures and text to clarify creation during the guided exploratory experience.

Grow

After establishing learning and skills in the guided project, further expand the depth of learning and the foundation of knowledge through an independent challenge. Through an independent challenge, a student maker takes on a challenge presented by the makerspace coordinator and creates something more complicated. The maker builds upon what was learned and the skills developed while creating during the guided exploratory experience. Included for each activity's independent growth experience is a creation challenge, websites to expand learning, lists of suggested equipment, supplies, and optional materials. In order to grow and learn to think independently, step-by-step instructions are not included. A student must work it out for himself, through trial and error as well as further research on the topic, in order to successfully complete the make.

Share

Each activity concludes with a list of suggestions for sharing learning and creations with the community.

Self-Directed Experimentation

Not included in each activity, but key to the evolution of learning, is a self-directed make. At this stage, the student is ready to set an independent goal. Learning continues through personal inquiry, designing and creating a product of personal choosing and design.

BEE BALM

My father, Ronald Burton, a retired analytical chemist, has developed the most fascinating hobby in his retirement: beekeeping. As he has grown more and more adept and well-respected in this hobby, I have grown intrigued by the uses of honey and beeswax, and the real and purported medicinal characteristics. Beeswax and honey are healthy ingredients in foods, but also commonly used, natural ingredients in lotions, soaps, and lip salve. Health remedies and kitchen uses of bee products can be traced back to beyond the time of the pharaohs and are ingrained in our psyche even today as alternative medicine for mind and body.

Contact the local beekeeping association for the needed beeswax, which may be donated, price reduced, or full price, depending on the situation. After the need and purpose is explained, the makerspace may have just found a mentor organization with which to partner. There are many recipes for making beeswax lip balm, so what is offered here is a place to start; then students could do some research into other ways to use beeswax, various ingredients, other ways of blending. They could create their own combinations and record their success and failures. Instructions below utilize a microwave, but very small slow cookers could also be used, depending on what is most convenient for the makerspace.

Let students experiment to find the perfect combination of texture, scent, flavor, and color. Environmental issues, like altitude and humidity, may have an impact, so experimenting is crucial. Accept failures as lessons learned, not roadblocks, until satisfied. Just as I tested various recipes, there was not one preferred, and I was instead most satisfied with the results of a blending of what was learned from trial and error, and taking the experimentation to construct a consistency and scent most preferred.

Think

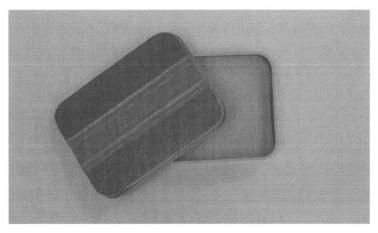

Learning and Building Knowledge

- American Beekeeping Federation. http://www.abfnet.org/index.cfm
- andersHQs kanal. "High Speed Summary of Life Inside the Beehive/Snabbspolning Genom Livet i Bisamhället." (video) http://www.youtube.com/watch?v=821uVRAcZ1I&feature=share&mid =53160
- Big Oven®. "A Kid's Guide to Honey—History, Recipes and More." http://www.bigoven.com/article /Recipe/kids-guide-honey
- Burns, Loree Griffin. *The Hive Detectives: Chronicle of a Honey Bee Catastrophe.* Houghton Mifflin Books for Children, 2010.
- Haagen-Dazs Loves Honey Bees. "The Honey Bee Crisis." http://www.helpthehoneybees.com /#crisisbee
- Food and Agriculture Organization of the United Nations: Agriculture and Consumer Protection Department. "Value-Added Products From Beekeeping." (Chapter 4: Wax) http://www.fao.org /docrep/w0076E/w0076e12.htm
- Frontier™ Natural Products Co-Op. "Baking Flavors and Extracts 101." http://www.frontiercoop .com/learn/features/bakingextracts101.php
- Mayo Foundation for Medical Education and Research. "Dry Skin Chapped Lips—What's the Best Remedy?" http://www.mayoclinic.com/health/chapped-lips/AN01440
- Renee Harris: hardlotion.com. "How to Make Lip Balms." (video) http://www.youtube.com/watch?v =YHEUC-m5wPQ

Create

Equipment: microwave, microwave-safe container, measuring spoons, small grater, measuring cups

Supplies: beeswax, scrap paper, wood craft stick, olive oil, coconut baking extract, recycled lidded metal tins (breath mint, tea, or small puzzle tins)

Optional Materials: scissors, box cutter, paper craft tape, alphabet stickers, sponge brush, Mod Podge®

Guided Exploratory Experience

Step 1. Clean and thoroughly dry tin. Set aside.

Step 2. Grate beeswax onto scrap paper.

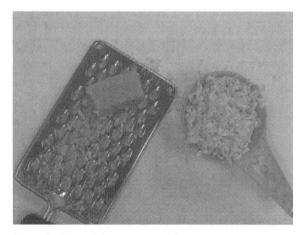

Step 3. Place ½ cup grated beeswax into a microwave-safe container.

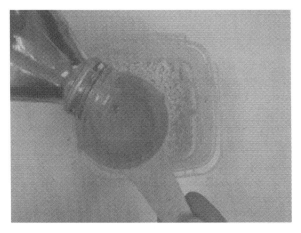

Step 4. Add ¼ cup oil and stir with craft stick.

Step 5. Microwave until melted. This is usually less than one minute, but melt time varies, depending on the microwave. Watch and stop microwave if it bubbles or boils. Stir.

Step 8. Allow ample time for lip balm to cool and set.

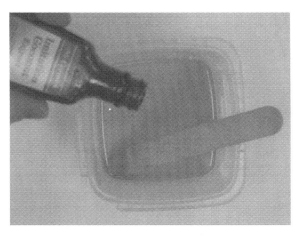

Step 6. Once melted, add ¼ to ½ teaspoon of baking extract and thoroughly stir.

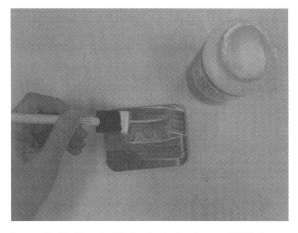

Step 9. Optional: While lip balm is cooling, decorate lid with paper tape and stickers, then seal with Mod Podge® (see Money Tin in Chapter 3)

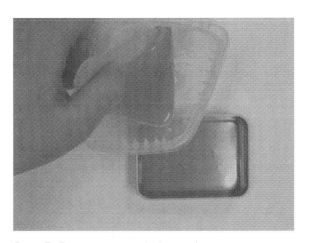

Step 7. Pour into recycled metal tin.

Grow

Independent Challenge

Experiment to create an ideal perfect combination of texture, scent, flavor, and color of lip balm.

Equipment: microwave, microwave-safe container, measuring spoons, small grater, measuring cups

Supplies: beeswax, scrap paper, wood craft stick, oil (sunflower, olive, coconut, jojoba, almond, etc.), baking extract (vanilla, coconut, almond, etc.), vitamin E capsules, shea butter, recycled lidded metal tins (breath mint, tea, or small puzzle tins), cake decorating glitter, cocoa powder, powdered drink mix in various colors

Optional Materials: paper craft tape, alphabet sticker, sponge brush, Mod Podge®

Learning and Building Knowledge

Discovery Communications. "Does Vitamin E Soothe Your Lips?" http://health.howstuffworks
    .com/skin-care/lip-care/tips/vitamin-e-soothe-lips.htm
Muchmann, Stephen. *Honey Bees: Letters from the Hive*. Delacorte Press, 2010.
NWNJBA: New Jersey Beekeepers Association (NJBA). "Making Lip Balm, Hand Cream,
    Beeswax Candles." (video) http://www.youtube.com/watch?v=QZheXsalYwo
Texas A&M University. "Honey Bee Information." http://honeybee.tamu.edu

Share

Use a desktop publishing program to produce illustrated recipe cards for display and distribution through the school library circulation desk and the front office welcome desk.

BODY SPRAY

· ·

Perfumes have a long history, dating back to the Assyrians, Ancient Rome, and a time when perfume was heavily used to mask the scent of unwashed bodies. Today, body scents are used less liberally and are a more discreet, subtle scent, but still used by both men and women.

It is easy to invest a lot in perfumes and colognes, but how hard would it be to make a scent custom suited? Actually, making a body spray isn't that difficult, but the challenge might be to find the right blend of fragrances.

Think

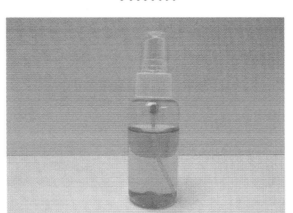

Learning and Building Knowledge

- American Society of Perfumers, Inc. http://www.perfumers.org
- eHow™. "How to Make Body Spray." (scroll down to the "Tips and Warnings") http://www.ehow.co.uk/how_5364701_make-body-spray.html
- PlantGuide.org. "Witch Hazel Tree." http://www.plantguide.org/witch-hazel-tree.html
- Roach, John. "Oldest Perfumes Found on Aphrodite's Island." National Geographic. http://news.nationalgeographic.com/news/2007/03/070329-oldest-perfumes.html?source=rss

Create

Equipment: measuring spoons
Supplies: vanilla essential oil or baking extract, witch hazel, distilled water, travel size spray bottle

Guided Exploratory Experience

Step 1. Take the top off the spray bottle.

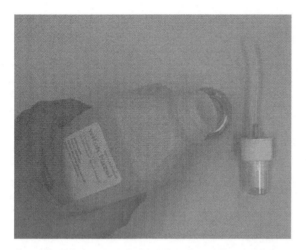

Step 2. Fill the bottle ¼ full with witch hazel.

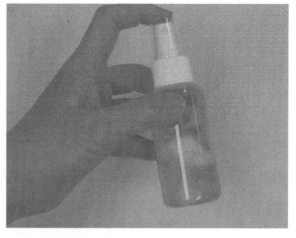

Step 4. Add ¼ teaspoon of essential oil or baking extract. Cover and shake.

Step 5. Allow to sit overnight before use.*

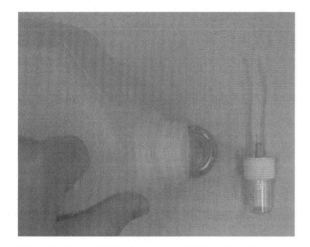

Step 3. Add distilled water until it is ¾ full.

---

* To test scent, spray toward wrist, then wait five minutes for the aroma of witch hazel to dissipate before smelling the wrist. Five to ten minutes after spraying, the true scent of the body spray will be apparent.

Grow

Independent Challenge

Customize a body spray scent to match the maker's personality and mood.

Equipment: measuring spoons

Supplies: wide variety of essential oils (chamomile, basil, clove, eucalyptus, ginger, lavender, lemongrass, olive, orange, peppermint, sage, spearmint, tea tree) and baking extracts (almond, anise, cinnamon, coconut, ginger, lemon, mint, orange, peppermint, vanilla), witch hazel, distilled water, travel size spray bottles

Optional Materials: glycerin

Learning and Building Knowledge

Stockstill, Elen. "10 Sources for Exotic Fragrances." TLC. http://tlc.howstuffworks.com/style /10-sources-for-exotic-fragrances.htm

University of Maryland Medical Center. "Aromatherapy." http://www.umm.edu/altmed/articles /aromatherapy-000347.htm

University of Minnesota. "Aromatherapy." http://www.takingcharge.csh.umn.edu/explore -healing-practices/aromatherapy

Share

Share the custom fragrance recipe with family and friends and show them how to make their own body spray.

COFFEE CUP COOKING

When cooking with students, I was shocked by how little students knew about the art of cooking and nutrition. Our initial goal was for students to learn, through experience, simple, affordable ways to make nutritious meals with minimal time. It was absolutely shocking that we needed to take a step back from our goal and spend time with adolescents practicing how to measure and follow the sequential steps in a recipe.

Part of the challenge for young people is portion control and a lack of interest in leftovers. That's when I started researching coffee cup cooking, which is single-serve cooking for the need-it-fast generation. In coffee cup cooking, a microwave is used and a single portion is prepared and cooked in the same small container, often a coffee cup but any microwave-safe container of similar size will do. Coffee cup cooking can be used for casserole-style cooking, desserts, and much more. For this make, students create a single-serving dessert, which was an amalgamation of many trial and error attempts of my own students. Key to the simplicity of this make is an angel food cake mix, which eliminates the need to add milk, eggs, or oil.

Think

Learning and Building Knowledge

- Dampier, Cindy. "Coffee Cup Cooking: Ingredients by the Drop, Cooking Times in Seconds Yield Instant Love-in-a-Cup." The Wichita Eagle, http://www.kansas.com/2012/04/17/2301171/coffee-cup-cooking.html
- *Healthy Eating: a Guide to Nutrition.* (Six volume set) Chelsea House, 2010.
- Mayo Clinic Weight Loss. "Slide show—Guide to portion control for weight loss." http://www.mayoclinic.com/health/portion-control/NU00267

Create

Equipment: microwave, food containers with lids, measuring spoons, microwave-safe coffee cup, spoon
Supplies: tape, "just add water" angel food cake mix, devil food cake mix, brownie mix, pudding mix, water
Optional Materials: butter knife, whipped topping, ice cream

Step 1. Open each mix and place it in an individual food container. Cut out the words describing what it is and tape to the lid.

Step 4. Add 1 teaspoon brownie mix.

Step 2. Measure 3 Tablespoons of angel food cake mix into a coffee cup.

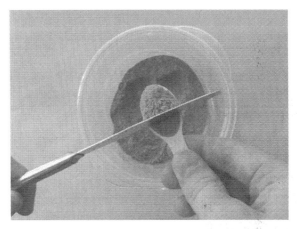

Step 5. Add ½ teaspoon of pudding mix.
Helpful Hint: For all powder measurements, scrape the flat side of a butter knife across the measuring spoon to remove the excess.

Step 3. Add 2 Tablespoons plus 2 teaspoons of devils food cake mix.

Step 6. Add 4 Tablespoons of water.

Step 7. Stir with a spoon until moistened, then stir another 50 strokes or until the appropriate consistence of cake batter.

Step 8. Turn spoon sideways and tap against the edge of the cup to drop excess back into the cup. Place in a microwave. Cook for one minute. Depending on the wattage of the microwave, add 30 seconds at a time until fully cooked without overcooking. It should be done when top looks spongy and when pressed lightly, it bounces back.

Step 9. Optional: Top with dollop of whipped topping or ice cream before eating.

Grow

Independent Challenge

Experiment with dessert recipes and create a delicious, single-serve mug variation.

Equipment: microwave, food containers with lids, measuring spoons, microwave-safe coffee cup, spoon

Supplies: "just add water" angel food cake mix, various cake mixes, various pudding mixes, other flavorings and textures (examples: nuts, small or crushed candies, miniature baking chips and morsels, jellies, coconut, oatmeal)

Other Supplies: other ingredients provided by students

Learning and Building Knowledge

Budget101. "Mug-Cup Mixes." http://www.budget101.com/frugal/mug-cup-mixes-193

Eating Well®. "Easy Healthy Cupcake Recipes." http://www.eatingwell.com/recipes_menus /recipe_slideshows/easy_healthy_cupcake_recipes?sssdmh=dm17.665202&esrc=nwdr 042713

Eating Well®. "Test Kitchen Secrets: How to Bake a Healthier Cupcake." http://www.eatingwell .com/healthy_cooking/kids_cooking/test_kitchen_secrets_how_to_bake_a_healthier _cupcake

Food.com™. "Mug Recipes." http://www.food.com/recipe-finder/all/mug

Recipe.com. "How to Make Cake Mix Cookies." (video) http://www.recipe.com/videos/v
/52034436/how-to-bake-a-cake-from-scratch.htm?sssdmh=dm17.665202&esrc=nwdr
042713

ThriftyFun™. "Coffee Mug Cake Recipes." http://www.thriftyfun.com/Coffee-Mug-Cake-Recipes
.html

United States Department of Agriculture. "Welcome to the USDA National Nutrient Database
for Standard Reference." http://ndb.nal.usda.gov

Yummly™. "Coffee Cup Recipes." http://www.yummly.com/recipes/coffee-cup

Share

Host a Coffee Cup Cooking demonstration day. Have students demonstrate to other students how to create their single-serving microwave meals and dessert.

COMICS AND GRAPHIC NOVELS

Comic books, graphic novels, and superheroes are everywhere, and are symbolic in American culture. Comic heroes have been absorbed into the way people think, process learning, and develop new thinking. Learning and entertainment today is a combination of text and visual. Studies have shown that reading graphic novels is valuable time spent reading. If this is the wave of knowing for the future, why not get students involved in the creative process?

Start by having students begin to understand the art of succinct writing with the story being told through two mediums: text and images. Play with setting up a three block comic strip to gather experience and proficiency, before moving on to a more in-depth novel and independent make.

Think

Learning and Building Knowledge

- BookRags. "Understanding Comics Summary." (study pack and lesson plans) http://www.bookrags.com/Understanding_Comics
- The Center for Cartoon Studies. http://www.teachingcomics.org
- Encyclopædia Britannica Online. "Comic Strip." http://www.britannica.com/EBchecked/topic/127589/comic-strip
- How to Draw Funny Cartoons. "Writing a Comic Strip in 3 Panels (or Less)." http://www.how-to-draw-funny-cartoons.com/writing-a-comic-strip.html
- McCloud, Scott. *Making Comics: Storytelling Secrets of Comics, Manga and Graphic Novels.* William Morrow, 2006.
- McCloud, Scott. *Understanding Comics: The Invisible Art.* William Morrow, 1994.
- ReadWriteThink. "Comic Vocabulary." http://www.readwritethink.org/files/resources/interactives/comic/vocabulary.html
- Roche, Art. *Comic Strips: Create Your Own Comic Strips from Start to Finish: Create Characters! Write Jokes! Get Published!* Lark Books, 2006.
- Universal Uclick. "Go Comics." http://www.gocomics.com/explore/comics

Create

Equipment: computer, Internet
Optional Materials: scanner, printer, printer paper

Guided Exploratory Experience

Step 1. Use Stripcreator to practice writing dialog and narration for three panel comic characters and setting.

Stripcreator: Make a Comic, http://www.stripcreator.com/make.php

Step 2. Go to Make Beliefs Comix® and construct three panel comic strips.

Make Beliefs Comix®, http://www.makebeliefscomix.com/

Step 3. Go to ToonDoo Maker and make a longer comic.

ToonDoo Maker, http://www.toondoo.com/

Step 4. Take random pictures of objects, the environment, and animals.

Step 5. Play with a free online photo editor, like befunky® or PicMonkey, to alter pictures and add text.

befunky®, http://www.befunky.com
PicMonkey, http://www.picmonkey.com

Grow

Independent Challenge

Prepare a problem-resolution storyboard and use it as an outline to design a graphic novel incorporating your own storyline, characters, setting, and digital photographs or artwork.

Equipment: computer with Comic Life 2, printer, digital camera

Supplies: paper

Learning and Building Knowledge

Candlewick Press. "Download a Toon Books Activity Kit." (page 8, "Games with Benny and Penny") http://www.candlewick.com/book_files/1935179012.kit.1.pdf

Candlewick Press. "Easy to Read Comics Toon Books Free Teacher's Resource." (page 29, "Problem and Resolution Organizer") http://www.candlewick.com/book_files /0979923816.btg.1.pdf

Free Comic Book Day. "Get Into Comics." http://www.freecomicbookday.com/Home/1/1/27 /986?articleID=116110

HarperKid's Channel. "How a Book is Made (with Lauren Oliver)." (video series) http://www .youtube.com/playlist?list=PLiYzMwyBPG953QtOwUP_cyfldfUltJym6

Heritage Auctions. "Comics Glossary." http://comics.ha.com/c/ref/glossary.zx

Paperwings. "How To Write A Comic Book Script and Other More Important Things." http://www.paperwingspodcast.com/2012/02/how-to-write-a-comic-book-script

Plasq. "Comic Life 2." http://plasq.com/products/comiclife2/win

Storyboard That. http://www.storyboardthat.com

wikiHow. "How to Write a Comic Book." http://www.wikihow.com/Write-a-Comic-Book

Share

1. Publish graphic novels and add graphic novels to the school library circulating collection.
2. Incorporate comic strips into the student newsletter or newspaper.

EMBROIDERY LOGO

Embroidery can be used to autograph and personalize a custom-made item. Consider the logos on sports bags, shoes, hats, and clothing. This is an opportunity for makers to create their own insignia, which can then be added to many of their makes. Embroidery can be done on many material types and with embroidery thread, yarn, or embroidery floss. For this experience, felt will be used due to its affordability and ease of use, but future embroidery makes could be done from any textile conducive to hand stitching.

In the guided exploratory experience, makers embroider on felt to make a small, scented satchel, which could be a good deodorizer for a locker or sports bag. The good smells from the satchel come from simply saving and re-purposing used, scented dryer sheets.

Does embroidery or quilting really take off in your makerspace? Would the school be interested in the makerspace creating spirit gear which the student makers sell as a makerspace or school fundraiser? Incorporating technology is important to STEM makerspaces, and the advanced computerized sewing and embroidery machines could be an interesting craftsmanship component.

Think

Learning and Building Knowledge

- About.com. "How to Sew: How to Thread a Needle." (video) http://video.about.com/sewing/How -to-Sew--How-to-Thread-a-Needle.htm
- Better Homes and Gardens® How to Sew.com. "How to Knot Thread." (scroll down to find "How to Knot Thread") http://howtosew.com/blog/sewing-basics/how-thread-needle
- Better Homes and Gardens® How to Sew.com. "Stitches to Know." http://howtosew.com/blog /sewing-basics/stitches-know
- Quilting in the Rain. "How to Tie Off a Blind Stitch." (video) http://www.youtube.com/watch?v= _SbFYoEgOh8

Create

Equipment: computer and printer, gently used cookie or sandwich cutter shape, scissors, embroidery needle (or appropriate gauge needle), ruler, straight pins, tweezers, unsharpened pencil

Supplies: printer paper, felt, used fabric softener dryer sheets, embroidery thread or yarn (weight category of 2 or less), tear-away stabilizer, new fabric softener dryer sheet

Optional Materials: small embroidery hoop

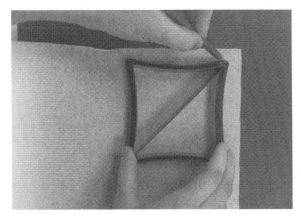

Step 1. Select the preferred sandwich cutter shape. Trace the shape with the pencil, then cut out the shape.

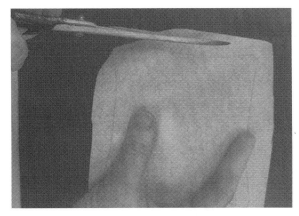

Step 2. Cut around the outside of the pattern, not yet directly cutting on the lines.

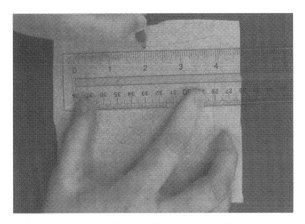

Step 3. Measure the width between the pencil lines, then divide in half. Mark that center measurement with the pencil on the line of both sides of the width. Draw a light line across the stabilizer to connect the dots.

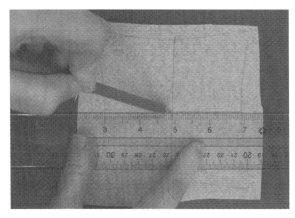

Step 4. Repeat Step 3 for the length. Where the two lines meet is the center.

Step 5. Use the computer and a word processing program. Alter the page margins to ½ to 1 inch less than the traced shape. For example, if the pattern is 4½ inches by 4½ inches, then the text space should be 4 inches by 4 inches. Select a desired, simple font and type the maker's first name on one line and last name on the second line. Center the text and print.

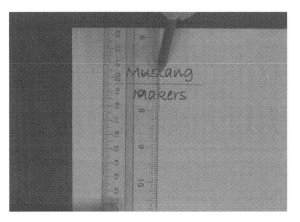

Step 6. As in Step 3 and Step 4, measure and mark the length and width to find the center point of the printed text.

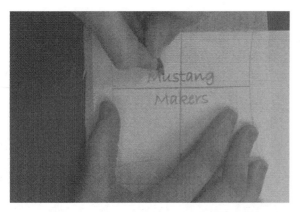

Step 7. Place the center point of the stabilizer on top of the center point of the letters. Rotate the stabilizer until the desired angle for the pattern is reached. Trace the letters with a pencil onto the stabilizer.

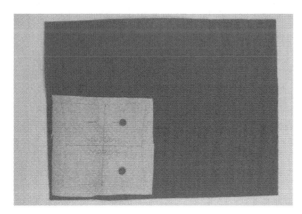

Step 8. Select a piece of felt long enough to double over and still cover the pattern on the stabilizer. Pin the stabilizer to two opposite edges of the felt, leaving enough room along the length so the felt can later be folded over to cut a front and back piece of the pattern.

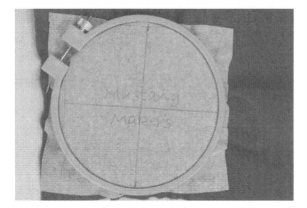

Step 9. Optional: Center the felt into an embroidery hoop to keep the felt stable.

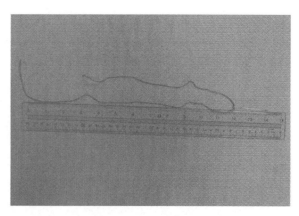

Step 10. Measure and cut a 24-inch length of thread or yarn and thread the needle. Tie a knot on the end.

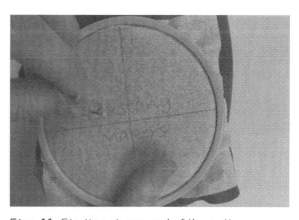
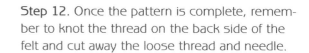

Step 11. Starting at one end of the pattern, use a *back stitch* to embroider the letters. If running low on thread, knot the end against the back side of the felt and rethread the needle as necessary.

Step 12. Once the pattern is complete, remember to knot the thread on the back side of the felt and cut away the loose thread and needle.

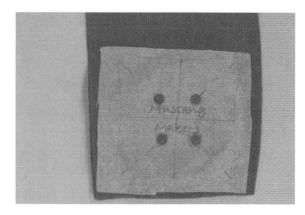

Step 13. If using a hoop, take the felt out of the hoop. Fold the felt over so the thickness of the felt is doubled. Use straight pins to secure the two pieces together.

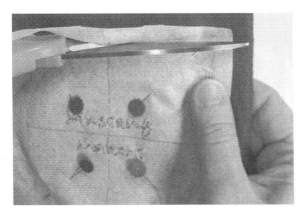

Step 14. While pinned together, cut the two pieces simultaneously. Cut along the pattern lines. This will be the front and the back of the satchel.

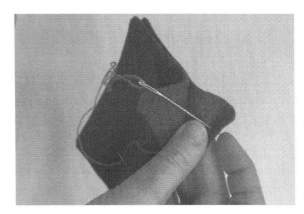

Step 18. Begin the first stitch on the inside so the knot will not be visible and carefully make even *blanket stiches* around the perimeter to sew the two pieces together.

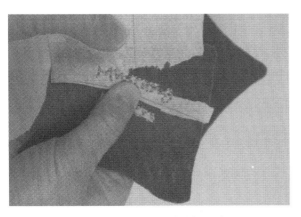

Step 15. Remove the pins. Holding the top piece only, remove the stabilizer. Pinch the stiches to keep the stiches from pulling as the stabilizer is tugged off. Use small scissors and tweezers to carefully pull away any leftover stabilizer from around the stitches without damaging the stitching.

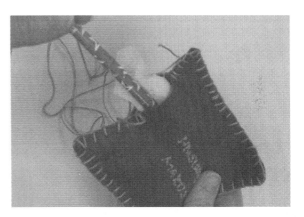

Step 19. While there is still ½ to ¾ inch of opening, pause the stitchwork. Use an unsharpened pencil to help stuff used dryer sheets into the center. Add one unused dryer sheet and continue until plump. Do not overstuff and strain the felt or stitches.

Step 16. Align the edges of the two pieces together again and repin the center.

Step 17. Thread the needle again and tie a knot on the end.

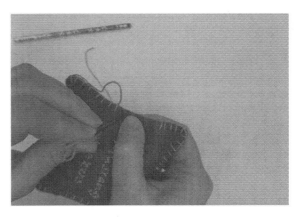

Step 20. Finish sewing, knot the thread, and cut the end. Use completed object as a deodorizer for a locker or sports bag.

Grow

Independent Challenge

Embroider a customized felt journal cover (see chapter 3).

Work with the available desktop publishing, or a free published pattern, or incorporate a combination of personal designs with professional designs. The pattern generated could be an embroidered design throughout the front of the journal cover or a personal logo in the corner.

Equipment: computer, printer, scissors, embroidery needle (or appropriate gauge needle), ruler, straight pins

Supplies: printer paper, felt, embroidery thread or yarn (weight category of 2 or less), tear-away stabilizer, pencil, tweezers, small embroidery hoop

Optional: desktop publishing program

Learning and Building Knowledge

Mary Corbet's Needle 'n Thread. "How to Videos." http://www.needlenthread.com/videos
Neeldecrafter.com. "Free Pattern Library." http://www.needlecrafter.com/patterns.html
Ray, Amy. *Doodle Stitching.* (series) Lark Books, 2007–2013.

Share

The maker uses the custom logo in a variety of formats, including electronic, as a brand for his many makerspace products.

FLOWER PRESSED DESIGNS

Cut flowers and greenery into pressed floral arrangements are a respected art form in many cultures throughout the world. Flowers are timeless and are used for many purposes: aesthetics, comfort, expressions of caring, aromatherapy, special events. Different blooms' colors have different connotation, different plants have different meaning, and different scents have different impacts on the human psyche.

Contact local florists in advance of the project until one is found who will donate their day old flowers and leaves or trimmings destined for the compost pile. Make arrangements to collect the donation as close to the makerspace project dates as possible. Or, is the makerspace in an area having an abundance of wildflowers? Contact appropriate property owners to request permission and arrange to hand pick flowers or blooming trees.

Flowers and leaves can be pressed and used in bookmarks, window decorations, ornaments, placemats, tile trivets and coasters, greeting cards, and other imagined endeavors. Flowers and leaves can be dried, but not flattened for preserved bouquets, potpourri, and much more.

Think

Learning and Building Knowledge

- Association of Specialty Cut Flower Growers. "Buy Local Flowers." http://www.ascfg.org/index.php ?option=com_content&task=view&id=118&Itemid=180
- Frost, Robert. *Poetry for Young People: Robert Frost*. Sterling, 1994.
- Pioneer Thinking. "The Language of Flowers-What They Mean." http://www.pioneerthinking.com /home/weddings/floral/flowerlanguage.html
- Poetry Foundation. "Spring Poems." http://www.poetryfoundation.org/article/241410?gclid=CKKgu -jhrLYCFXSVMgodzVwA5g
- teleflora®. "The Color of Flowers." http://www.teleflora.com/flowercolors.asp

Create

Equipment: iron, ironing mat, hole punch, ruler, scissors, pencil
Supplies: small flowers and leaves, clear contact paper, recycled paper, masking tape, yarn or thin ribbon
Optional Materials: paper trimmer, tweezers

Guided Exploratory Experience

Step 1. Set up ironing board or mat. Drain any water out of iron and turn to low.

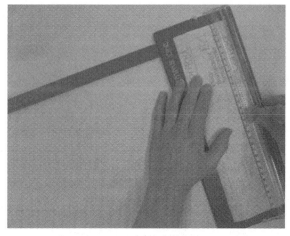

Step 2. Measure and cut a piece of contact paper, 3 x 12–14 inches.

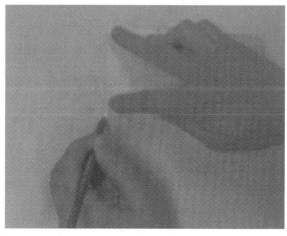

Step 4. Trace the outline of the folded contact paper onto the clean side of a piece of recycled paper.

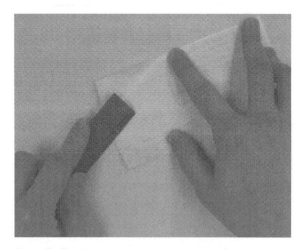

Step 3. Fold the contact paper in half, with the contact film facing out. Carefully align edges and corners. Use a ruler to press down and crease the center.

Step 5. Select small flower petals and leaves.

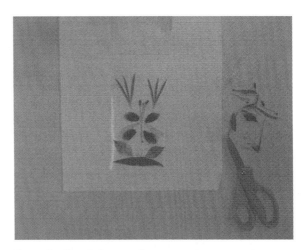

Step 6. Use the traced outline to lay out a design. Use scissors to trim leaves and petals as desired for a successful pattern. Shape off tips or ends of bulbous areas. Leave space in the pattern at the top center for a hole punch. Maintain a safe margin, keeping everything away from the edges. Do not excessively overlap flowers or leaves.

Step 7. Carefully peel the paper backing off the contact paper to expose the sticky side. Peel it back to the crease line.

Step 9. Carefully use fingers or tweezers to transfer the flowers and leaves, moving the pattern onto the sticky contact paper. Gently smooth each piece into place with a fingertip.

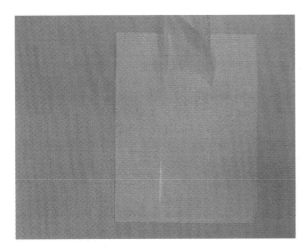

Step 8. Lay the contact paper down, sticky side up, on recycled paper. Tape down the contact paper, just above where the sticky contact paper is exposed to hold the unexposed piece in place.

Step 10. Remove the contact paper from the recycled paper. Lay it back down, peel away the backing from the top a little bit at a time, slowly pressing it into place on top of the other half of the contact paper, sealing the two sides together.

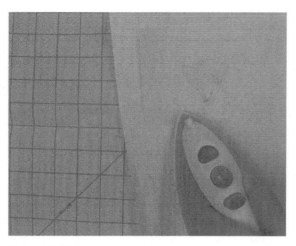

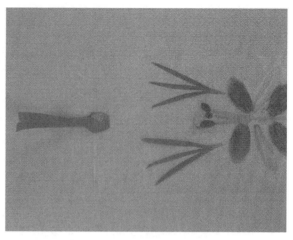

Step 11. Place a piece of recycled paper under the project and one on top. Move the papers and project to the ironing mat. Press and wiggle the iron over the project, then set aside to cool.

Step 12. While it is cooling, select and cut a 6 to 9 inch piece of yarn or ribbon.

Step 13. Punch a hole into the top center of the bookmark with the hole punch, avoiding any petals or leaves.

Step 15. With just a little bit of yarn or ribbon sticking out of the hole, fold the ends through the loop and pull gently on the ends to close the loop.

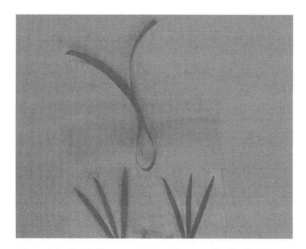

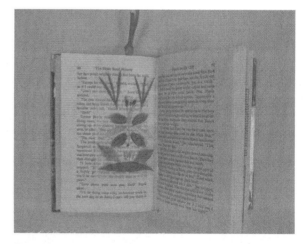

Step 14. Fold the yarn or ribbon in half. Push the loop end through the hole.

Step 16. Place in a book as a bookmark.

Grow

Independent Challenge

- Utilize a weeded book, book press, or microwave flower press to press flowers, leaves, and petals, then use the pressed flowers to create a personal design for a picture frame, greeting card, or other purpose of the maker's choosing.

- Equipment: weeded books (thick), scissors, tweezers
- Supplies: flowers and leaves, recycled tissue paper, other items as needed or provided by the individual
- Optional Materials: Book Press, Microwave Flower Press, cardstock and envelopes

Learning and Building Knowledge

- MonkeySee®. "How to Press Flowers." (video) http://www.monkeysee.com/play/14402-how-to-press-flowers
- MonkeySee®. "Preparing Flowers to Press." (video) http://www.monkeysee.com/play/14404-preparing-flowers-for-the-press
- *Peterson Field Guides.* (series) Houghton Mifflin Harcourt.
- Purdue University. "Senior Study-Flowers and Indoor Plants." http://www.hort.purdue.edu/ext/senior/flowers/flowers.htm
- Wildflower Identification. http://www.realtimerendering.com/flowers/flowers.html
- ThriftyFun™. "Drying Flowers." http://www.thriftyfun.com/Drying-Flowers.html

Share

After researching and testing other ways to utilize preserved flowers and leaves, create an instruction guide for others to follow for a project and pattern of the makers own creation.

GAME TILES

• •

There is a STEM strength to playing tile games, which include the traditional Dominos, Mah-Jongg, Rummikub®, Mexican Train, Rummy Tile, Pai Gow Dominoes, Tri-Ominos®, and now there are a range of popular computerized variations of tile games. Tile games have a long history throughout the world. Each have their own origin story and many have traveled across continents and oceans to be adapted to fit the interest and experiences of a new culture. For example, although Mah-Jongg is of Chinese descent, there is now an American version. The games require strategy, math skills, and a complicated set of rules to remember and process throughout every move.

Begin with a simple double six Domino set. Once proficient in the game, try creating a tile game which is more complex to make and to play, like American Mah-Jongg.

Think

Learning and Building Knowledge

- Andalusia Rotary Club. "World Championship Domino Tournament." http://www.worlddomino.com
- Domino-Games.com. "How Many Tiles and Dots Are In A Dominoes Set?" http://www.domino -games.com/faq/How-Many-Tiles-And-Dots-Are-In-A-Dominoes-Set.html
- Domino-Games.com. "The History of Dominoes." http://www.domino-games.com/domino-history .html
- eHow™. "How to Play Dominoes." (video series) http://www.ehow.com/videos-on_4391_play -dominoes.html
- NTDTV. "Human Mattress Dominoes" World Record in Shanghai." (video) https://www.youtube .com/watch?v=NIRT_95dsGs
- ShanesDominoez. "8,000 Dominoes—Disney Motion." (video) https://www.youtube.com/watch?v =tcUIK-tkzlI&list=UUOX63bpgBCd0kg7MWgU20wg&index=2

Create

Equipment: sponge brush, ruler, pencil, computer, printer

Supplies: 28 laminate countertop tile samples, old newspaper, paper correction liquid, black spray paint, newsprint, resealable plastic bag, Mod Podge® (sparkle, flat, or glossy), printer paper

Optional Materials: rocks

Guided Exploratory Experience

Step 1. Take old newspaper outside with black spray paint and 28 laminate countertop tile samples to make a Double Six Domino set. If a Double Nine, Twelve, Fifteen, or Eighteen is desired, more tiles will be needed.

Step 2. Lay the newspaper out on the ground. Place rocks down on the corners to hold the newspaper in place. Lay the tiles in a single layer, upside down, on the newsprint.

Step 3. Follow the directions on the spray can and spray the back surfaces of the tiles. Take care about wind direction, otherwise the painter may get flecks of paint on clothing.

Step 4. Allow time to dry.

Step 5. Lay dried tiles, painted side up, on a newsprint covered work surface.

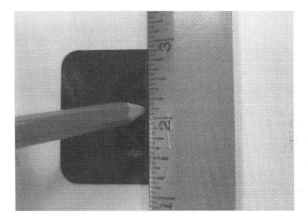

Step 6. Measure the width of the tile. Make a straight line down the center of the tile with the ruler and pencil.

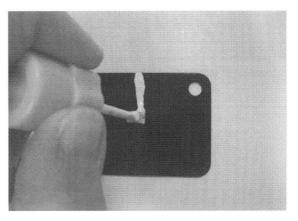

Step 7. Carefully paint over the line with the paper correction fluid brush. Repeat for all tiles. Allow to dry.

Step 8. Examine the appropriate place for a dot on each tile (zero to six dots) as required to make a complete Double Six Domino set.

Step 11. Research rules and how to play the game. Use a word processing or desktop publishing program to type simplified how-to-play instructions and rules in an easy to understand manner. Use any fonts, copyright free clip art, and borders desired.

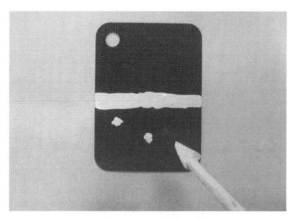

Step 9. Before working on the tile, practice on the newsprint making dots with the paper correction fluid. Once ready, place a dot as appropriate on each tile to make the domino game set. Allow time to dry.

Step 12. In between playing games, place the guide sheet and tiles in a resealable plastic bag and seal shut.

Step 10. Protect the paper correction fluid. Use a sponge brush to coat the tile with Mod Podge®. Set aside to dry. Repeat the process as directed on the container, brushing in an opposite direction for each new coat.

Grow

Independent Challenge

Students examine the history and game fundamentals for Mah-Jongg (or other preferred tile game), make an American Mah-Jongg game set, then learn to play.

Equipment: paintbrush, sponge brush, cup with clean water

Supplies: 152–166 laminate countertop tile samples, paint (blue, green, red), white spray paint, newsprint, resealable plastic bag, egg crate for paints, Mod Podge®

Additional Playing Supplies: dice, paper, pencil, tile holders

Learning and Building Knowledge

The American Mah-Jongg Association. http://www.amja.net

Board Games Central. "Mah Johngg." http://www.boardgamecentral.com/games/mj.html

Mahjong-games. "American Style Mahjong Rules." http://mahjong-games.awardspace.biz /images/american-mahjong-rules.pdf

North American Mahjong Federation. American Style Mahjong Rules." http://www.mahjong federation.com/American-Style-Mahjong-Rules.html

Sandberg, Elaine. *Winning American Mah Jongg Strategies: A Guide for the Novice Player.* Tuttle Publishing, 2012.

Sandberg, Elaine and Tom Sloper. *Beginner's Guide to American Mah Jongg: How to Play the Game & Win.* Tuttle Publishing, 2007.

Sloper, Tom. *The Red Dragon & The West Wind: The Winning Guide to Official Chinese & American Mah-Jongg.* William Morrow, 2007.

Yellow Mountain Imports. "American Mahjong." http://www.ymimports.com/t-howtoplay_amj .aspx#Introduction

Share

1. Donate the completed domino game to a local family shelter. Include a personal note about how the game was made and how to play.
2. Host a Tile Games game day.
3. Host learning days where students use their games to teach other students the rudiments of the game.

KITE FLYING

Kites are an inexpensive and a deceptively simple pastime. A vivid childhood memory is attending a summer day camp where we built, decorated, and flew our own kites. It was such a fantastic experience to make something that actually flew. I remember holding a friend's kite while he prepared to make his run to catch the wind and get his kite in the air. The beauty of watching everyone's kite go up at once, going higher and higher, wiggling in the wind, was a powerful moment.

Making a kite that can remain airborne and be maneuvered by a simple string from the ground is more complicated than it seems. To construct an efficient kite, knowledge of the principles of gravity, friction, and motion are necessary.

A kite is a familiar idea. Most youth have heard of a kite and although most have heard of kites, many youth today have no experience flying kites. Building kites into the makerspace incorporate STEM and creativity into the thinking process.

Think

Learning and Building Knowledge

- American Kite Flyers Association. http://aka.kite.org
- Gomberg Kite Productions International, Inc. "Kites as an Education Tool." http://www.gomberg kites.com/nkm/index.html
- KTAI Kite Trade Association International. "Kite History and Fun Facts." http://www.kitetrade.org /page.asp?id=6
- National Kite Month®. "How to Run a Kite Workshop." http://www.nationalkitemonth.org/teachers /runworkshop.php
- NASA. "Kite Index, Glenn Research Center." http://www.grc.nasa.gov/WWW/K-12/airplane/shortk .html

Create

Equipment: miter box and saw, craft knife, ruler, pencil, scissors

Supplies: two lightweight wooden rods (sticks, balsa, or dowel), bulletin board Kraft paper rolls or large trash bag, kite string, old ties

Optional Materials: empty toilet or paper towel roll, twine

Guided Exploratory Experience

Step 1. Wooden dowels or balsa wood can be purchased, but if the local environment permits, have makers hunt for and bring their own straight, wooden sticks.

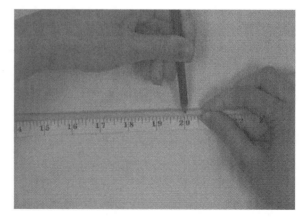

Step 2. Measure and cut the shorter stick to 20 inches.

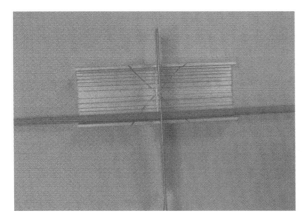

Step 3. Measure and cut the longer stick to 24 inches.

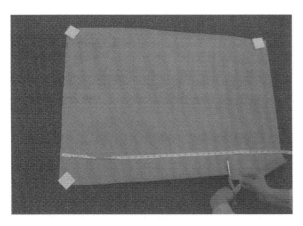

Step 4. Cut a 26 x 26 square of bulletin board paper or trash bag.

Step 5. Optional: If the makerspace is not purchasing a class set of kite string or the maker is not providing his own, kite string can be made by rolling 200 feet of twine onto a toilet paper roll or onto one end of a paper towel roll.

Step 6. Follow steps one through twelve of the instructions at PBS.org's Benjamin Franklin: Make a Kite website: http://www.pbs.org/ben franklin/exp_kite.html.

Step 7. As Step 13 on the online instructions suggests, knot a length of string 2 yards long to the bottom for the tail.

Step 8. Take apart and open up ties. Cut pieces into 10 inch long sections.

Step 9. Cut the strips again to make about nine long, narrow ribbons.

Step 10. Tie the ribbons to the tail approximately every 8 inches.

Step 11. Test kite. Adjust tail according to need for successful flying. Add ribbons if difficult to control. Remove ribbons if too heavy.

Grow

Independent Challenge

Construct an aerodynamic kite of personalized shape and design, adding decoration and design.

Equipment: craft knife, ruler, pencil, scissors, miter box and saw

Supplies: permanent markers or other lightweight decorating supplies

Learning and Building Knowledge

Morgan, Paul and Helene Morgan. *The Ultimate Kite Book: The Complete Guide to Choosing, Making, and Flying Kites of All Kinds-From Boxex and Sleds to Diamonds and Deltas, from Stunts*. Simon & Schuster, 1992.

National Kite Month®. "Kite Fun for Kids: How to Fly a Kite" http://www.nationalkitemonth.org/kids/howtofly.php

Share

1. Host a kite flying event, festival, or family day.
2. Analyze kite designs to understand which are more efficient for getting off the ground, which fly highest, and which can be to maneuvered while flying.
3. Create templates and instructions for others to replicate successful kites designed by the makers.

LOOM KNIT

It began with finger knitting and my elementary age daughter, Paige, showing me how she learned to finger knit. My daughter proved that knitting is for everyone when she stayed focused on her self-imposed challenge and made finger-knitted garland for a six foot Christmas tree. What made finger knitting so great was that it brought knitting to the average person. Knitting is a pastime that is popular, crosses gender lines, and continues today. The sense of satisfaction one gets at the visible progress and sense of accomplishment is instantaneous. Even more proof that knitting is here to stay is the fact that a fabulous language arts teacher in my school, Erin Nieten, hosts a successful knitting club who call themselves the Knit Wits.

Shortly after my daughter's introduction to finger knitting, a co-worker and talented artist, Denise Britt, invited me to a yarn shop to sit in on a knitting session. I admit, I was an abysmal failure at traditional knitting, but I so wanted to knit, especially after I saw all the colorful and innovative yarns. That's when I was introduced to something similar in principle to finger knitting called loom knitting, which has made knitting accessible to even me, the most inept at hand to eye coordination.

In the exploratory experience, makers create their own single knit loom, then a bookmark. It's simple, cost effective, and good for short attention spans. If students like loom knitting, the small, single knit loom could be reused to create other things.

Think

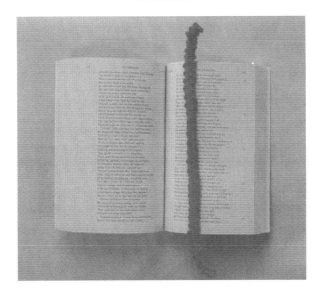

Learning and Building Knowledge

- All Free Knitting. "Knitting Tutorial-How to Make a Slipknot." http://www.allfreeknitting.com /Knitting-Tutorials/Knitting-Tutorial-How-to-Make-a-Slip-Knot#
- Interweave™ Craft. "Knitting Dailt TV Yarn Spotlight, Episode 1001 - Made in America." (video) https://www.youtube.com/watch?v=PYN5wSHR6Vs
- Lion Brand® Yarn. "Loom Knitting: How to Bind Off for Single Knitting." (video) http://www.you tube.com/watch?v=O15nZhF7I1M
- Lion Brand® Yarn. "Loom Knitting: How to Cast On for Single Knitting." (video) http://www.you tube.com/watch?v=xcx-OeiN090
- Lion Brand® Yarn. "Loom Knitting: How to Knit." (video) http://www.youtube.com/watch?v=U4Lk _Uo581U

- Loom Knitting. "Loom Knitting Terminology." http://www.loomknitting.com/pages/definitions.htm
- Loom Knitting Videos. "Free Loom Knitting Video Tutorials and Patterns for Beginners and Pros." http://loomknittingvideos.com

Create

Equipment: miter box and saw, ruler, pencil, yarn needle

Supplies: yarn, paint stir stick, narrow wood crafts sticks, craft glue, permanent marker, duct tape, safety pin

Optional Materials: resealable plastic sandwich bag, colored narrow wood craft stick

Guided Exploratory Experience

Make a Single Knit Loom

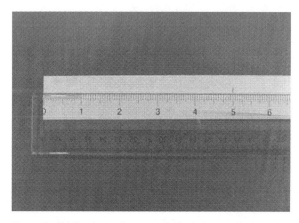

Step 1. With the ruler, mark 5 inches off the paint stir stick. Cut along the mark with the miter box and saw.

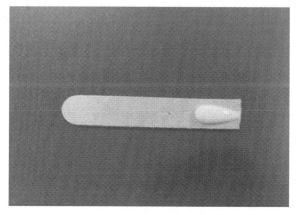

Step 3. Toward the mitered end of one craft stick piece, place a small strip of glue.

Step 2. Use the miter box to cut three narrow wooden craft sticks in half. Cut one colored craft stick in half, or draw lines with permanent marker on both sides of a plain wooden craft stick.

Step 4. Place the stick, glue side down, centered at two and a half inches, with the mitered end flush with the base of the stir stick.

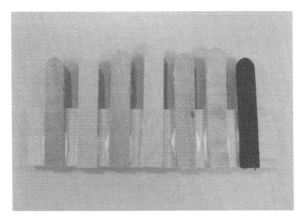

Step 5. Glue three of the stick halves, each ¼ inch apart from the next, to the left of the center craft stick. Then, glue three cut sticks to the right of the center sticks, using the colored craft stick for the last stick on the right.

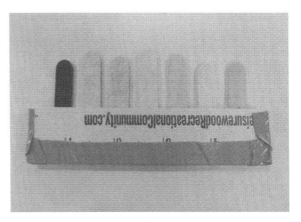

Step 7. Turn it over and wrap the tape around, pressing it into place.

Step 6. To reinforce the glued placement of the craft sticks, cut six inches of duct tape, center it on top of the sticks along the base. Line the top edge of the length of the tape with the top edge of the stir stick. Press the tape into place.

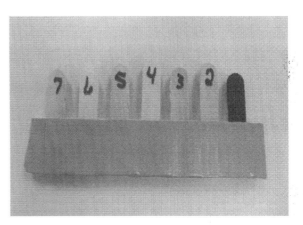

Step 8. Number the top of the sticks with the permanent marker, *from right to left*, 1 through 7. The craft sticks are now *pegs* and the paint stir stick is now the *base* of the single knit loom.

To Make an Oval Loom: To make an oval loom, cut two 6 inch strips from the stir stick plus six ½ inch blocks. Make, glue, and tape the sticks on as instructed above. Glue three of the blocks together, then the other three. Turn the loom over to the back side (opposite of the sticks) and glue one block set to the far edge of one end, then the other set to the other edge and finally, glue the 6 inch strip on top (this should leave an opening in the center for the knitted yarn to drop through). If desired, tap nails into the ends to reinforce the hold. Wrap duct tape around the base of the loom, overlapping slightly. This is now a small oval loom.

Single Knit Loom Bookmark

Step 1. Measure and cut 200 inches of yarn. Roll into a ball.

Step 2. Optional: Place ball into a resealable plastic sandwich bag with the tail of the yarn hanging out of one corner. Seal all but that corner. This will help keep the yarn clean and controlled.

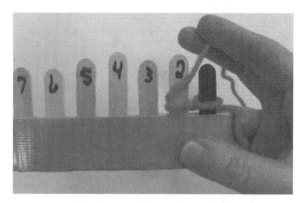

Step 5. Loosely wrap the yarn, counter-clockwise, twice around peg two.

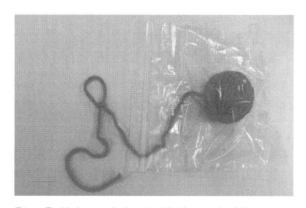

Step 3. Make a *slipknot* with the end of the yarn.

Step 6. Using a finger and thumb, pinch the bottom yarn loop. Bring the bottom loop on peg two over the top loop and lift it up and over to the back of the peg, then push the yarn to the bottom of the stick.

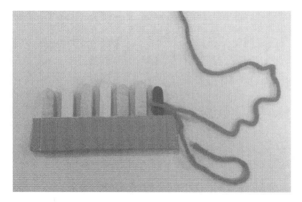

Step 4. Place the slipknot loop on colored peg one.

Step 7. Repeat Step 5 and Step 6 for peg three. Do not pull the yarn too tight or it will become difficult to get the yarn over the pegs.

Step 8. Now the yarn needs to go back to the right, so bring the yarn across the front of peg three and between peg three and two. Hold the yarn between two fingers to hold it behind the loom.

Step 11. To go back to the left, bring the yarn across the front of peg two and between peg two and three. Again, hold it behind the loom and bring the bottom loop on peg two over the top loop and lift it up and over to the back of the peg. Push the yarn to the bottom of the stick.

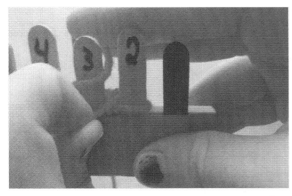

Step 9. Using pinched fingers, bring the bottom loop on peg three over the top loop and lift it up and over to the back of the peg. Push the yarn to the bottom of the stick.

Step 12. Repeat the steps to continue knitting back and forth. Once there is about 1 inch of knitting hanging out the back, release the slip-knot from the colored peg one.

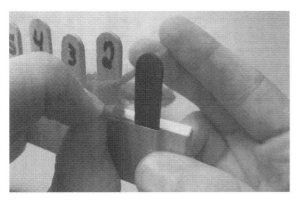

Step 10. Repeat Steps 8 and 9 for peg two.

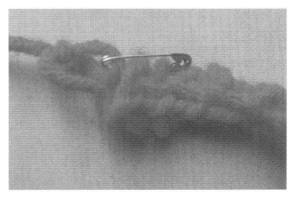

Step 13. Pin the slipknot to a knitted section of yarn for safekeeping.

Step 14. Optional: When not working on the knitting, place the loom in the bag with the yarn. Remove it again when ready to continue, paying close attention to where the knitting was stopped and needs to begin again.

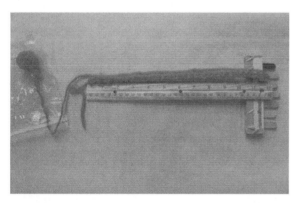

Step 15. Continue to knit until the knitted bookmark is 12 inches long, or the length the maker prefers for a bookmark. Be sure to stop knitting where the knit began, at peg two.

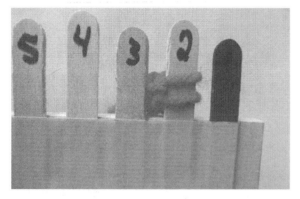

Step 16. Pull the loop off peg three and place it over peg two.

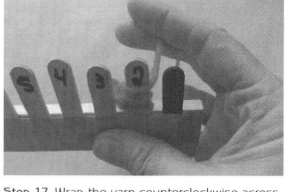

Step 17. Wrap the yarn counterclockwise across peg two.

Step 18. Pinch the bottom two loops and lift them up and over to the back of the peg.

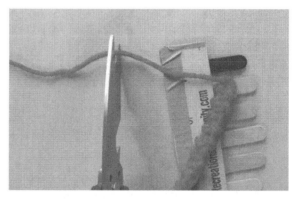

Step 19. There is now only one loop left on peg two. Cut off the excess yarn, leaving a 3 inch tail of yarn.

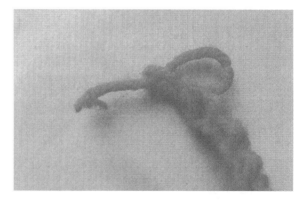

Step 20. Pull the loop off peg two, then bring the tail of yarn through the loop.

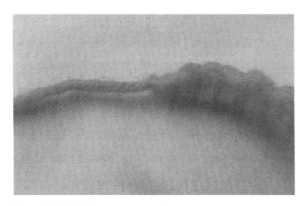

Step 21. Pull gently to tighten into a knot.

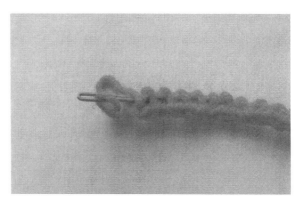

Step 23. Hide the yarn by sewing it through the length of the bookmark to secure it.

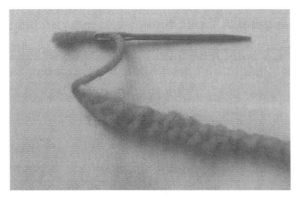

Step 22. Thread the tail of yarn through a yarn needle.

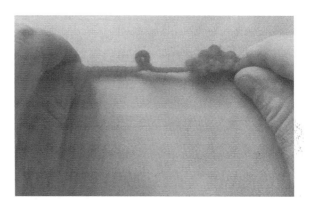

Step 24. Remove the safety pin and slipknot from the other end. Repeat Step 23.

Grow
Independent Challenge

- Design and create a skinny scarf or cowl.

- Equipment: Knifty Knitter knitting loom, loom hook, yarn needle

- Supplies: yarn

Learning and Building Knowledge

House of Humble. "On Being a Man Who Knits." http://www.houseofhumble.com/2011/12/on-being-a-man-who-knits

Lion Brand® Yarns. "Free Loom Patterns." http://www.lionbrand.com/cgi-bin/patternList.fcgi?tXX=1&s=loom&l=1

Norris, Kathy. *Big Book of Loom Knitting: Learn to Loom Knit.* Leisure Arts, 2012

Provo Craft & Novelty. "Introduction to Knifty Knitter®." (video) http://www.provocraft.com/video

Provo Craft & Novelty. "Knifty Knitter®."http://www.provocraft.com/products/index.products.php?cl=knifty%20knitter

Ravelry. https://www.ravelry.com/account/login

Share

Create and distribute an instruction guide for others to follow a knitting pattern created by a maker.

MUSIC COMPOSER

Music is an absorbing component to the lives of adolescents. It's on the radio, on their phone, on the Internet, in movies, integral to television programs, and so much more. Many students enjoy participating in a choir, band, or orchestra through school, church, clubs, or privately. Playing and creating music expands the passive listening to actively engaging in the music process. Making music incorporates so many skills including, but not limited to, sound patterns, mood, tone, and storytelling.

If songwriting really takes off in the makerspace, consider investing in an advanced songwriting tool, like MasterWriter: http://masterwriter.com/songwriters.html for independent challenges.

Think

Learning and Building Knowledge

- Audacity®. http://audacity.sourceforge.net
- Audacity®. "Manuals and Documents." http://audacity.sourceforge.net/help/documentation
- Datamuse. "Rhyme Zone." http://www.rhymezone.com
- Hammond–Olivares, Marisa. "Tone and Mood Words." (video) http://www.youtube.com/watch?v=jDUhDV-7250
- Latenight. "Jimmy Fallon, Carly Rae Jepsen & The Roots Sing "Call Me Maybe" (w/ Classroom Instruments)." (video) http://www.youtube.com/watch?v=lEsPhTbJhuo
- *New Oxford Rhyming Dictionary*. Oxford University Press, 2012.
- Pattinson, Pat. "Verse Development." The Muse's Muse. http://www.musesmuse.com/patart.html
- Watson, C.J. *Essential songwriting: everything you need to compose, perform, and sell great songs*. Adams Media, 2006.

Create

Equipment: computer, microphone, microphone headset, rhyming dictionary, printer, word processing program, audio recording and editing software

Supplies: paper

Optional Materials: household and office items for inventing instruments or student provides his own instruments

Guided Exploratory Experience

Step 1. Write song lyrics.

Step 2. Construct a music composition to fit the mood and tone of the lyrics, utilizing the student's instrument or household items.

Step 3. Record composition in Audacity® or other preferred audio recording and editing software.

Step 4. Edit as needed, then publish final song as an MP3 or other preferred format.

Grow

Independent Challenge

Write song lyrics, then use Notation Composer software, or other preferred software, to create sheet music for various instruments which supports the mood and tone of the lyrics. Practice, then digitally record using Audacity®, Jam Studio, or other preferred program.

Equipment: computer, microphone, microphone headset, rhyming dictionary, printer, word processing program, audio recording and editing software

Supplies: paper

(Makers provide or make their own instruments and provide their own band)

Learning and Building Knowledge

Chord Studio, Inc. "Jam Studio." http://www.jamstudio.com/Studio/index.htm
Hitsquad Musician Network. "Hitsquad Music Software." http://www.hitsquad.com/smm
Notation Software™. "Music Notation Software for Everyday Musicians." http://www.notation
 .com/NotationComposer.php
Scott Made This. "BeetBox." http://scott.j38.net/interactive/beetbox/
SherryCNotation channel. "Notation Software Tutorial Series." (video) http://www.youtube.com
 /user/SherryCNotation?feature=plcp

Share

1. Play students' final masterpieces as background music in the makerspace.
2. Host a makerspace Music Composer concert.
3. Enter a song written, performed, and produced by teens into a songwriting competition, like the International Songwriting Competition: http://www.songwritingcompetition.com/ or The John Lennon Songwriting Contest http://www.jlsc.com/index.php.

PAPER QUILTING

A creative alternative to the expenses of fabric quilting is paper quilting. Australian artist Michaela Laurie transformed the art of quilting with the conversion of the art form from fabric to paper. Paper quilting brings the creativeness and aesthetic beauty of quilting and transfers the concept to gift tags, greeting cards, and framed art.

My mom, Rochelle Burton, is an amazing quilter. She invests a lot of time and money into her award-winning quilts. She taught me many things about quilting and how quilting has modernized to make it more fun and efficient. There are sewing machines which contain small computers and are programmable; computerized sewing machines, fabric cutting systems, rotary cutters, and cutting edge rulers, just to name a few, have revolutionized the art.

Unfortunately, the fabric and high-end machines, which could make quilting so interesting to young people, also make fabric quilting financially impossible for many school makerspaces.

Even so, if paper quilting (and DIY couture) becomes popular in the makerspace, seek grants, donators, and creative funding to purchase a computerized sewing machine. A quality sewing machine is an equipment investment, so research carefully to find the one to best fit the makerspace needs. Among the sewing machine manufacturers respected by quilters are Singer®, Brother®, Janome®, Bernina, and Viking®.

Think

- Better Homes and Gardens® How To Sew.com. "How to Thread Your Sewing Machine." (video) http://howtosew.com/blog/sewing-basics/how-thread-your-sewing-machine
- Indiana 4-H Youth Development. "4-H Sew Much Fun: Helper's Guide." Purdue University. (Glossary, pp. 16–19) http://www.extension.purdue.edu/extmedia/4H/4-H-929-W.pdf
- Indiana 4-H Youth Development. "Mini 4-H Sewing Project." Purdue University. (Practice Stitching Guide, p. 8) http://www3.ag.purdue.edu/counties/stjoseph/Documents/NEW%202012-%20Mini %20Sewing%20Manual.pdf
- Paper Quilting 10. "How to Make a Paper Quilt Gift Tag." (Video) http://www.youtube.com/watch ?v=9lmkJye3Ss8
- Singer. "Operation Basics." http://www.singerco.com/sewing-resources/operation-basics
- University of Florida. "Florida 4-H." (Sewing Machine Parts and Basic Threading Guides, p. 4) http://florida4h.org/projects/fcs/clothing/files/Clothing_Capers/CC_Lesson1.pdf

Create

Equipment: sewing machine (with zigzag stitch), ruler, pencil, scissors, narrow patterned decorative edge scissors, paper cutter

Supplies: newsprint, printer paper, various thread colors, bobbin with white thread, used greeting cards, craft glue stick, A2 size envelope, cardstock, spray adhesive, glossy page from a weeded book

Optional Materials: fine tip marker

Guided Exploratory Experience

Step 1. Lay newsprint down on the workspace, then go through used greeting cards until the preferred image to repurpose for the front of a paper quilt card is chosen.

Step 2. Use the paper cutter to cut the image down to 4 x 3 inches.

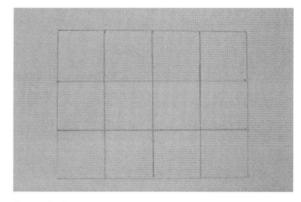

Step 4. On a half sheet of printer paper, use the ruler and pencil to outline a 4 x 3 inch rectangle. Then, add lines in the rectangle to make twelve 1 inch squares. This is the paper quilt template.

Step 3. Cut the rectangle into 1 inch squares.

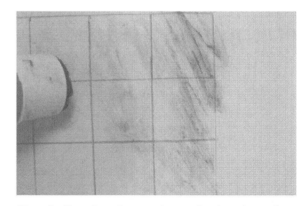

Step 5. Use the glue stick to rub glue throughout the template.

Step 6. Place the image squares from the cut-up rectangle into the template as if putting together a puzzle until all pieces are glued in place. Allow glue to dry.

Step 7. Select a thread color to accentuate the image. Thread the sewing machine. Set the sewing machine to zigzag stitch.

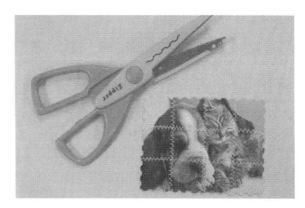

Step 10. Select a pair of decorative scissors. Cut out the perimeter of the quilt while cutting on the inside seam so that all exposed pieces of the template are cut off. Keep cut lines as straight as possible.

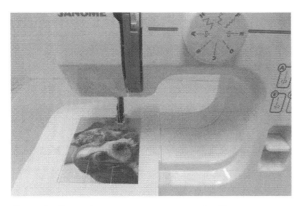

Step 8. Sew the inside seams only. Starting on the template paper before the quilt squares, and ending on the paper after the last quilt square, sew the length of the longest inner seam.

Step 11. Use the center of a glossy page from a weeded book for the paper quilt's mat. Tear the page out of the book, turn it at an angle on the paper cutter, and cut a 4¼ x 3¼ inch rectangle of text.

Step 9. Repeat to sew the next long inner seam, then turn the paper and zigzag stitch together the remaining inner seams.

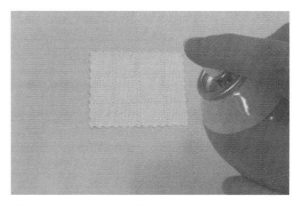

Step 12. Place the quilt piece upside down on newsprint, or other scrap paper large enough to protect the work surface. Follow the instructions on the spray adhesive can to spray the back of the paper quilt. Do not over-spray.

Step 13. Cautiously pick up the paper quilt, turn it over, and place it, centered, on the mat. Press and smooth out the quilt onto the mat. The two pieces should now be glued together. Set aside to dry.

Step 16. Consider the pattern on the quilt and how the card will open. Lay the matted quilt on the front of the card until desired placement is decided. Holding in place with one hand, gently lift a corner and mark lightly on the card with a pencil under the edge of each of the four corners.

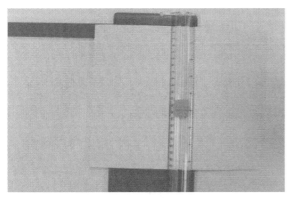

Step 14. Begin to make the card. Use the paper cutter to cut the width of a piece of cardstock in half.

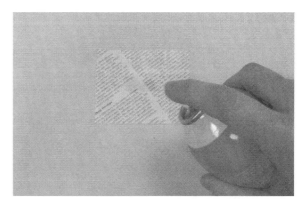

Step 17. Place the matted quilt piece upside down on newsprint, or other scrap paper large enough to protect the work surface. Follow the instructions on the spray adhesive can to spray the back of the paper quilt. Do not over-spray or the paper may wrinkle.

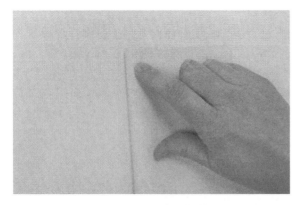

Step 15. Fold the cut piece in half lengthwise and press down the seam. This is the card.

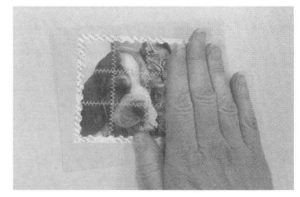

Step 18. Cautiously pick up the matted quilt, turn it over, and carefully place it on the card, using the pencil markings as a guide. Press and smooth out the quilt onto the card. Allow time to dry.

Step 19. Optional: Turn the card over. Using a fine tip marker, make a "created by" signature on the back.

Step 20. Use a pre-made A2 envelope or make an envelope with solid color scrapbook paper or white printer paper following the instructions for envelopes (see Chapter 3).

Grow

Independent Challenge

Begin with a computer-drawing program. Design artwork that looks like a simple coloring-page-style with just simple lines separating major shapes. Use the artwork to create a paper quilt pattern and make a paper quilt with scrapbook paper scraps for framed art.

Equipment: computer, printer, drawing software, sewing machine (straight and zigzag stitch), scissors, decorative edge scissors

Supplies: thread and bobbin, solid sheets of scrapbook paper, decorative scrapbook paper (partials and scraps), glue stick, cardstock

If there is no drawing program available in the makerspace, research possible programs or consider these options: Artweaver Free http://www.artweaver.de/download-en/, ArtRage4 http://www.artrage.com/artrage-4.html

Learning and Building Knowledge

Michaela Laurie Paper Quilt Creations. "Questions-Making a Paper Quilt." http://paperquilt
creations.blogspot.com.au/p/questions-making-paper-quilt.html

Shackelford, Anita and Jennifer Perdue. *Teens & Tweens: Quilting with Family and Friends.*
AQS Publishing, 2009.

SHOPS @ McCall. "Paper Quilt Creations by McCall's Creates." http://shops.mccall.com/about
-paper-quilt-creations-pages-3516.php

Stegmiller, Terri. *Creative Paper Quilts: Applique, Embellishment, Patchwork, Piecework.* Lark
Books, 2009.

Share

Create a sharable book for the makerspace of maker's templates for custom designed paper quilt patterns.

PLARN WEAVING

Have plenty of grocery bags, bread bags, dry cleaner bags, and other plastic bags? There is use for all of those plastic bags. Collect plastic bags and sort and store them by color until needed, then make plarn from the sorted pile. Plarn is plastic yarn. Plastic yarn is homemade yarn made out of plastic bags. Plarn can then be used to traditionally knit, crochet, loom knit, finger knit, weave, and braid.

Just as yarn comes in different thicknesses, plarn can be made in a range of thicknesses, depending on how fat the plastic strips are cut. The plarn can then be used for a variety of projects, including jewelry, dog leashes, rugs, bookmarks, placemats, totes, jump ropes, and much more.

For a first experience with plarn, try weaving a travel seat, which could be used for sitting upon outdoors and at sporting events.

Think

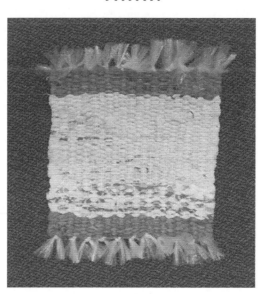

Learning and Building Knowledge

- craftstylish®. "How to Weave on a Cardboard Loom." http://www.craftstylish.com/item/2546 /how-to-weave-on-a-cardboard-loom/page/all
- EPA. "How Do I Recycle . . . Common Recyclables." http://www.epa.gov/recycle/how_recycle .html#pla
- It's Our Environment EPA's Blog About Our World. "Plastic Bags Are Everywhere, What Can We Do?" http://blog.epa.gov/blog/2008/07/plasticbagsareeverywhere

Create

Equipment: scissors, box cutter, ruler, tape measure, pencil, cutting mat
Supplies: plastic grocery bags, paper box lid, dry cleaner bags

Guided Exploratory Experience
Making Plarn

Step 1. Sort plastic bags by color.

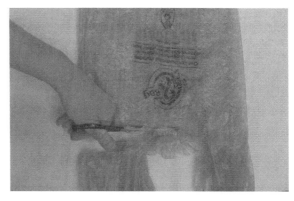

Step 5. Cut the bag along the handle side to cut off the handles and even out the top.

Step 2. Tuck the puckered seam in and smooth out each bag.

Step 3. Make a uniform stack of a few straightened bags.

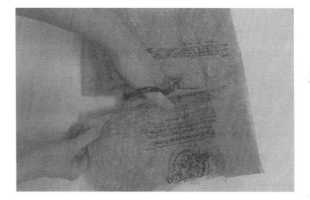

Step 6. The bags now need to be cut into strips. Thickness depends on the project. For the outdoor seating mat, a thick plarn is needed, so cut the bags in half, for about 6 inches fat, or thickness. Note: the smaller the project, or the smaller the desired weave, the thinner the strips should be cut.

Step 7. To weave the cut pieces together into plarn, make an open loop of one piece.

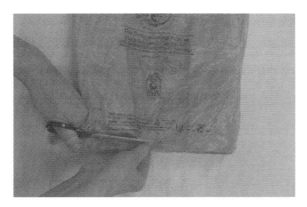

Step 4. Simultaneously cut the bottoms off the bags.

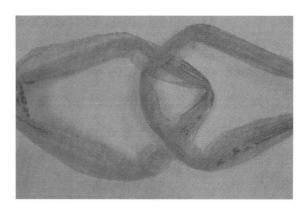

Step 8. Slide another looped piece under one end of the first piece.

Step 9. Slide a hand under the far end of the second piece, through the opening in the center, over the end of the first piece, to grab the opposite end of the second.

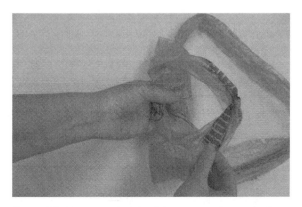

Step 10. Keeping hold of the opposite end of the second piece, pull the hand back through.

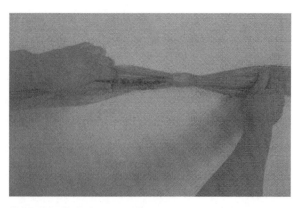

Step 11. Pull, bracing the pieces and keeping it straight, to tighten the knot. If the knot is accidentally off sides, just loosen the knot, slide it to the center, and retighten.

Step 12. Repeat process until the desired amount of plarn is created.

Step 13. Roll plarn into a ball, just as traditional yarn, and set aside until needed.

Make a Loom for Weaving

Step 1. Break open the seams and lay flat a paper box lid or other flat cardboard on a cutting mat.

Step 2. Using a ruler or other straight edge to maintain a straight line, cut one end off of the lid, along the seam line, with a box cutter.

Step 3. Decide the length and width needed for the travel seat. The example uses seventeen inches by seventeen inches, but size will depend on the person. Use the tape measure, measure up from the straight edge created

in step two, mark off the measurement a few times across the top.

Step 4. Use a ruler and pencil to connect the marks into a straight line. Cut with a box cutter.

Step 5. Repeat for the remaining sides until desired size square has been cut.

Step 6. Once the desired size is cut, use a ruler to mark off one-half inch below the width. Connect the marks to make a straight line.

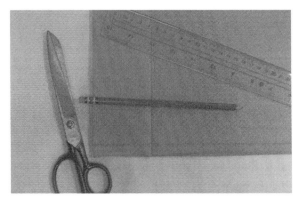

Step 7. Along the line, make a hash mark every ¾ inch. Make sure there are an even number of marks.

Step 9. Make identical triangles directly opposite. Repeat Steps 6, 7, and 8 on the opposite side. The completed board is now the *loom*.

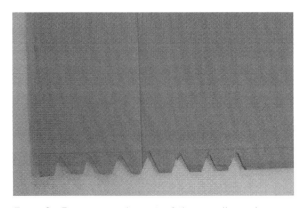

Step 8. Cut a triangle out of the cardboard, using the hash mark as the triangle's point. Repeat to complete the length.

Weave a Travel Seat

Step 1. Make a ball of 4 inch fat plarn out of four dry cleaner bags.

Step 2. Begin stringing the loom. Loop the dry cleaner bag plarn over the first notches at the top and bottom of the loom and turn the loom over.

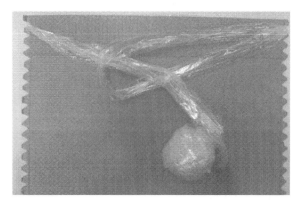

Step 3. Loop the ball through the plarn end and pull tight.

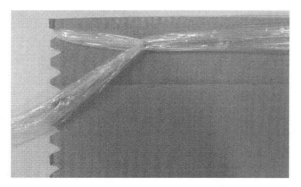

Step 4. Pulling the plarn in the opposite direction of the tied loop to keep it tight, begin wrapping the dry cleaner plarn around the loom into the triangle notches.

Step 5. Once the loom has been fully strung, turn the loom over to the back side. To tie off, look for a knot in the plarn on the back of the loom a row or two in and on the opposite end from where the plarn stopped. Pull the end of the plarn to that selected knot to measure. Cut the extra plarn approximately six inches past the chosen knot.

Step 6. Pull one end of the loose plastic through the knot.

Step 7. Pull both ends tight, and double-knot the ends of plastic together, using the knot on the loom as a placeholder for the knot.

Step 8. Approximately one inch from the knot, cut off the excess plastic.

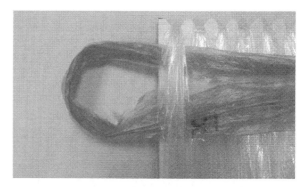

Step 9. To begin weaving, turn the loom over so the front is facing up. Cast on a length of plarn approximately seven feet long by placing one end of the desired color of a six-inch-fat plarn under the top of the first string on the loom.

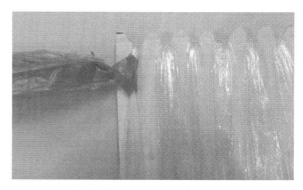

Step 10. Just as when making plarn, make a hoop out of the end, bring the rest of the plarn through the hoop, and pull it through straight and tight to knot onto the top corner of the first string.

Step 11. Taking the loose end of the plarn, place it over the next string, under the third string, and continue the over-under pattern until the far end is reached.

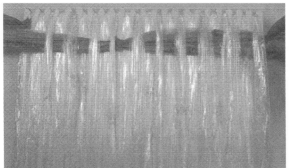

Step 12. Pull the excess plarn through the weave. Once nearly all the plarn has been pulled through, hold the looped end of plarn down on the string with one hand. This will keep you from pulling too tight. Tug the yarn at the other end to pull it snug. It is important not to weave too tight. If the weave is pulled tight, the weave will develop narrow and uneven edges.

Step 13. With fingers, push the weave snugly against the line above. As the weave progresses, it will be possible to re-tighten the weave. It is a good idea to go back through the weave periodically to pull, pinch, and re-tighten rows.

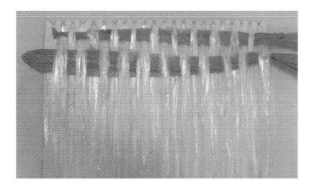

Step 14. Take the end of the plarn and weave back through the strings in the opposite manner; if the plarn went under a string for the last row, it goes over the string for this row. Continue taking the yarn over and under the string to the end of the row.

Step 15. Repeat Steps 11–13 until the weaving is complete. Continue to tighten as the weave progresses. Connect more lengths of plarn as needed or to change colors.

Step 16. When the desired length of the weave has been reached, cut off the excess plarn, leaving an extra 6 inches on the end.

Step 17. Take the end of the plarn and place one piece under the last string and one piece over the string.

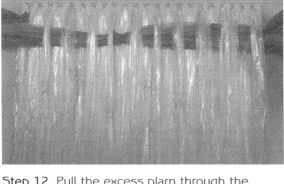

Step 18. Tie it to the string using a double knot.

Step 19. Cut off the excess.

Step 22. Turn the loom back over, cut the next two strings. Turn it over to the front and tie the next set of strings together for each end.

Step 23. Repeat Steps 20, 21, and 22 until all the strings have been cut and tied.

Step 20. Turn the loom over. Cut the first two strings.

Step 24. Cut off the excess tails of the strings 1 inch from the knot for the fringe.

Step 25. Optional: If no fringe is desired, cut closer to the knots.

Step 21. Turn the loom back over. On one end of the weave, double-knot the tails of the two strings together. Repeat for the other end of the loose strings.

Grow

Independent Challenge

Work in teams to weave a 3 x 5 sleeping camp mat.

Equipment: scissors, box cutter, ruler, tape measure, pencil, cutting mat

Supplies: fat plarn (approximately twelve inches fat) from estimated 500–600 plastic bags for each mat, donated cardboard (like from a refrigerator box) 5½ feet tall or larger, dry cleaner bags cut into 6 inch wide plarn for the strings

Learning and Building Knowledge

Homeless Resource Exchange. "Resources for Homeless Persons." http://www.hudhre.info
/index.cfm?do=viewHomelessResources

Homeless Shelter Directory. http://www.homelessshelterdirectory.org

ThriftyFun: Plastic Bag Rug. http://www.thriftyfun.com/tf517076.tip.html

Share

Coordinate work with a community center to donate the sleeping mats to the homeless.

PUZZLED INSPIRATION

Working on completing a puzzle is a lost art for some students. When I brought out puzzles and laid them out in the school library, I was amazed by how many students could not remember ever working on putting together a puzzle in the past. Working puzzles is great problem-solving for the brain. The problem with puzzles, though, is lost pieces. Once a puzzle piece is lost, don't throw away the puzzle, but instead save it for other projects. In the guided example, makers create a piece of art, painting and gluing puzzle pieces together before adding an inspirational quote in artful lettering.

Think

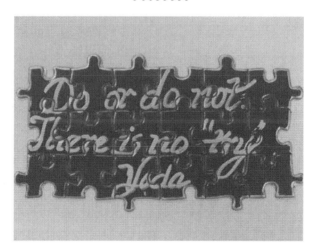

Learning and Building Knowledge

- American Jigsaw Puzzle Society. "History of Jigsaw Puzzle." http://www.jigsaw-puzzle.org/jigsaw-puzzle-history.html
- Bartleby.com. "Quotations." http://www.bartleby.com/quotations
- *Bartlett's Familiar Quotations.* Little Brown and Company, various editions.
- Donley, Marci and DeAnn Singh. *Hand Lettering: Simple, Creative Styles for Cards, Scrapbooks & More.* Lark Crafts, 2009.
- *Lettering: In Crazy Cool Quirky Style.* Klutz, 2006.
- ml4macdo. "1000 Piece Jigsaw Puzzle Time-Lapse (Photomosaic)." (video) http://www.youtube.com/watch?v=pep4VbPiZ-o
- Ostrom, Lindsay and Vicky Breslin. *Kid's Book of Creative Lettering.* Cut-It-Up, 2001.
- Values.com® The Foundation for a Better Life®. "Inspirational Quotes." http://www.values.com/inspirational-quotes

Create

Equipment: scissors, quote books and websites, sponge brush, pencil, variety of colors of fine point permanent markers

Supplies: old puzzles, spray paint, adhesive backed sheet (felt, contact paper or vinyl paper), newsprint, Mod Podge®

Optional Materials: magnet, ribbon, industrial hole punch, rocks

Guided Exploratory Experience

Step 1. Put together a puzzle until there is a section approximately 3 x 5 inches. Only use inner pieces; no edge or corner pieces.

Step 2. Take the puzzle pieces, plus a couple extra pieces, newsprint, and spray paint outside. Lay the newsprint on the ground. Take the puzzle section and extra pieces and lay the pieces face up on the newsprint. Place rocks on the corners of the newsprint to keep it from moving. Follow the instruction on the can to spray paint the puzzle pieces until all the image is covered by the paint. Allow time to dry.

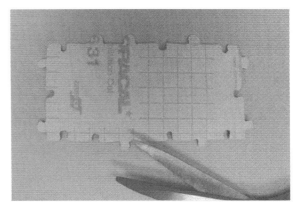

Step 6. Cut out the outline inside the traced line.

Step 3. Once dry, put the puzzle back together. Keep the extra puzzle pieces to the side.

Step 4. Place the adhesive sheet upside down on the workspace, so the adhesive backing is facing up.

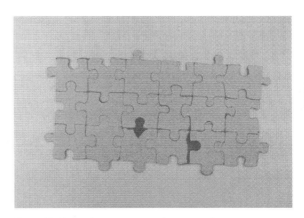

Step 7. Turn the put-together puzzle section upside-down.

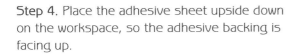

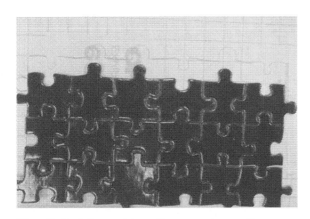

Step 5. Set the put-together puzzle section on top of a corner of the sheet and trace the outline onto the sheet backing.

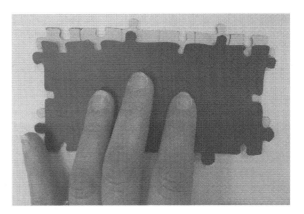

Step 8. Without removing the glue backing, carefully place the cut sheet on the puzzle, adhesive-side touching the back of the puzzle. Arrange until lined up correctly. Trim as necessary to better fit.

Step 9. Peel back a small section of backing to expose the adhesive. Press adhesive directly onto the back of the puzzle. Once secure, hold down the glued section. While peeling the backing toward the opposite direction, small sections at a time, press down the new section as you go. Continue until all backing is secured to the puzzle.

Step 10. Make a loose fist and rub with the back of fingers across the full area to better secure glue in place.

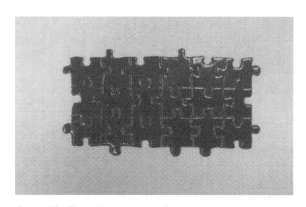

Step 11. Turn the project face-up on newsprint.

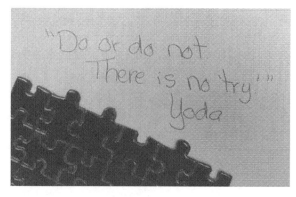

Step 12. Finalize selection of a quote to place on the puzzle surface. Write the quote and attribute onto the newsprint.

Step 13. Make final selection of calligraphy or font style to use. Practice the style on the newsprint.

Step 14. Select a permanent marker color. Test it on one of the extra puzzle pieces to make sure the ink will be visible and have the desired effect.

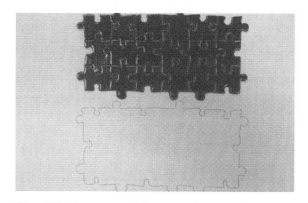

Step 15. Use a pencil to trace the puzzle section outline onto newsprint. Practice with the permanent marker laying out the quote and author in the selected writing style. Repeat tracing the outline and painting the print until satisfied with the appearance.

Step 16. Once satisfied, begin writing on the puzzle, using the newsprint pattern as a guide.

Step 17. Optional: Use a permanent marker; this could be the same color as the quote or a new color to make a border. If using a different color, first test the new colors on the scrap puzzle piece.

Step 18. Trace back over the letters with the marker as needed to smooth out the color. Set aside to dry.

Step 19. Following the directions on the Mod Podge® container, use a sponge brush to brush on a sealant. When laying the next coat, brush in the opposite direction.

Step 20. Put the artwork on display. This could be done by adding a magnet to the back for a locker or refrigerator decoration, or tack it to a bulletin board, or punch out a hole to add a piece of ribbon for a bookmark or wall hanging, or use another display idea suggested by the maker.

Grow

Independent Challenge

Consider spatial design while creating a wall hanging. Select one powerful, long word. Lay painted puzzle pieces at random angles, not connected or put together, into a shape outline, like a square, diamond, triangle, heart, trapezoid, or octagon which also seems appropriate to the selected word. Glue a second layer of painted puzzle pieces on top of the first layer, again laying the pieces at odd, random angles. Make sure the size is perfect to ensure the exact number of the exposed puzzle tiles is equal to the number of letters in the selected word. Once dry, spray paint the shape. Consider how the shape will hang and therefore, which tile to start the word, and then write one letter of the word on each tile.

Equipment: thesaurus, dictionary, pencil, variety of colors of fine point permanent markers

Supplies: puzzle pieces, craft glue, ribbon or yarn, newsprint, spray paint

Optional Materials: industrial hole punch, rocks

Learning and Building Knowledge

The American Heritage Roget's Thesaurus. Houghton Mifflin Harcourt, 2013.

JigZone.com™. http://www.jigzone.com

Merriam-Webster®. "Dictionary Thesaurus." http://www.merriam-webster.com

Stewart, Martha. "All About Jigsaw Puzzles with Anne Williams." (video) http://www.martha
 stewart.com/910410/all-about-jigsaw-puzzles-anne-williams

Share

Use children's-size small puzzle, which has been prepared and painted to match the mood and tone of the poem, as the mat. Write a funny or uplifting poem to paint on it. Send as a get well card to the children's wing of a local hospital.

RECYCLED BEADING

Beads are decorative components to jewelry, shoes, jackets, clothing, bags, keychains, and so much more used by men and women. Beads could be made from glass, plastic, gemstones, wood, stone, cloisonné, paper, metal, seeds, seashell, crystal, cloth, clay, and pewter.

In my youth I was blessed to spend time with Aunt Rita. Everyone should have had an "Aunt Rita." She was always kind, calm, smiling, and made every person feel as if they mattered. Every visit, she would spend time with us kids. During one visit, when I was twelve years old, she taught me how to make beads with a toothpick, bit of glue, string, plastic beads, and the covers of old church bulletins she had saved. It is a memory I cherish of my aunt, mother, and my brothers and sister sitting around a table rolling strips of paper into works of art. It was upcycling decades before the word upcycling came into power. I still wear jewelry we made that day, thirty years ago. The beads still look as good as the day we made them.

The width of the fat end of the paper will help determine the fatness of the bead and what is made with the bead. Approximately three-fourths an inch wide is good for a bracelet or earrings and one inch width for a necklace, keychain, zipper pull, or other object.

Think

Learning and Building Knowledge

- Beading-Design-Jewelry. "Symbolic Meaning of Colors." http://www.beading-design-jewelry.com /symbolic-meaning-of-colors.html
- Haab, Sherri and Michelle Haab. *Jewelry Upcycled!: Techniques and Projects for Reusing Metal, Plastic, Glass, Fiber, and Found Objects.* Potter Craft, 2011.
- HowStuffWorks. "How Magazine Printing Works." (video) http://www.youtube.com/watch?v=0g EEaFT5z84
- Paper University. "Recycled Paper Beads." http://www.tappi.org/paperu/art_class/paperbeads.htm

Create

Equipment: scissors, paper trimmer, sponge brush
Supplies: weeded hardback fiction book, toothpicks, craft glue, egg carton, cotton swabs, old glossy catalog, Mod Podge®, hemp cord, pony bead, 4 MM round beads with a hole size the same or slightly smaller than the homemade book beads, larger or longer beads with the same hole size as the round beads

Guided Exploratory Experience

Making Fiction Book Beads

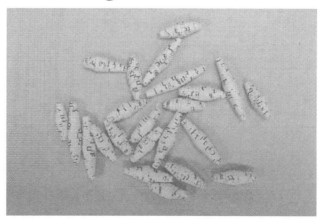

Step 1. Take an old fiction book apart so that all is left is the inner pages.

Step 3. Make strips of paper so that it is fat on one end and comes to a centered point at the other, like a long triangle. To begin, align the length of the trimmed page so that one corner is on the cut line and the other is ³/₈ inch, or half the desired bead width, over the edge. Trim and discard the straight-edged end piece.

Step 2. Take one page from the center of the book and use the paper trimmer to trim off the margins from all four sides. The text should be at the edges of the paper.

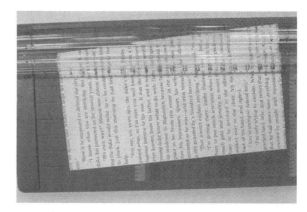

Step 4. Do the opposite angle. Hold the edge of the page against the cut line just created in Step 3. Move the opposite end of the page to ¾ over the edge. The point should be centered, with both sides as evenly angled as possible. Slide the blade to cut the triangle.

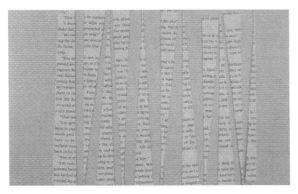

Step 5. Do the next angle by moving the opposite end of the paper (than was moved in step four) and leaving the other end against the cut line and cut.

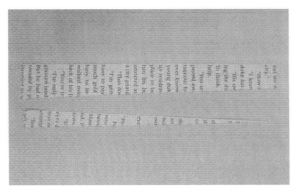

Step 6. Repeat this zig-zag cutting pattern until triangle strips have been made from as much of the page as possible. Discard the straight-edged end piece.

Step 7. Repeat Steps 2–6 until the desired amount of triangle strips have been cut.

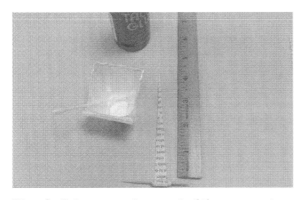

Step 8. Cut one egg base out of the egg carton and squeeze a little bit of craft glue into the bottom. Set the rest of the carton aside for later.

Step 9. Tear a glossy page out of an old catalog for a work surface. Lay a triangle strip on the page.

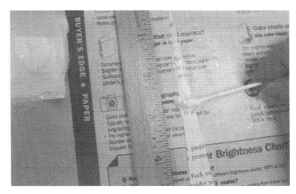

Step 10. Dip the end of cotton swab into the glue. Brush the glue along the last 3 inches of the pointed end of the triangle. Brush the glue past the edges and onto the catalog page to be sure all of the end is coated.

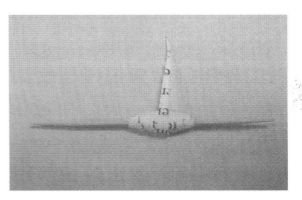

Step 11. Center the opposite wide end onto a toothpick and begin tightly rolling toward the glue.

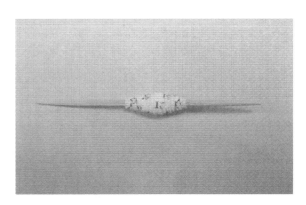

Step 12. Keep an eye on the sides as rolling to make sure it is not rolling lopsided and the glued tip will be fairly centered in the middle of the completed roll.

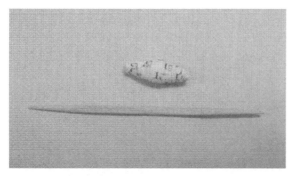

Step 13. Pull the completed bead off the toothpick and repeat Steps 10–12 until all beads have been rolled. If the catalog page work surface gets too sticky, replace it with a new one. Allow time for all beads to dry.

Step 15. Stick the opposite end of the toothpick into the top of the egg crate.

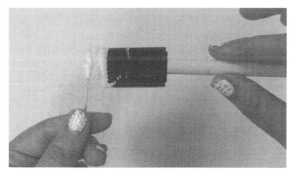

Step 14. Rest a bead on the end of toothpick. Do not push it down. With a sponge brush, brushing toward the grain, or the direction of the roll of the bead, seal the bead with Mod Podge®.

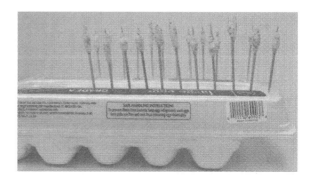

Step 16. Repeat Steps 14 and 15 until all beads are coated. Allow time to thoroughly dry.

Step 17. Remove dried beads from toothpicks.

Making a Unisex Choker Necklace

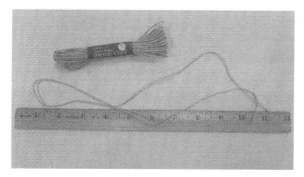

Step 1. Cut a 24 inch length of hemp cord.

Step 5. Select the round beads and larger beads to string with the fiction book beads. Cut another section of egg carton in which to place and sort the beads.

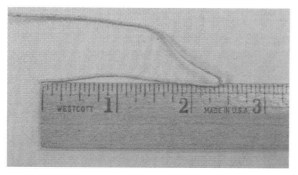

Step 2. Fold 2½ inches of cord over.

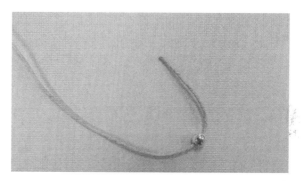

Step 6. String a round bead first and pull it down the cord to the knot.

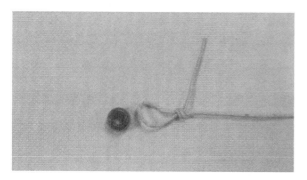

Step 3. Make a loop knot large enough for a pony bead to fit through. Make the knot tight.

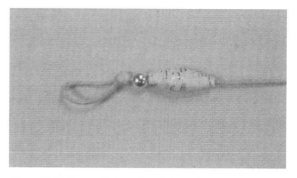

Step 7. String a fiction book bead next.

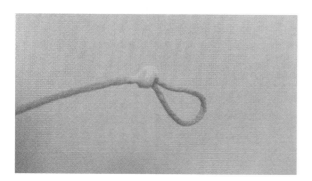

Step 4. Cut off the excess cording, then rub glue into the knot. Allow time to dry.

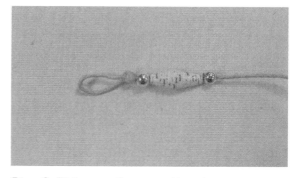

Step 8. String another round bead.

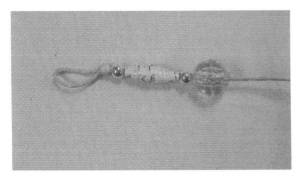

Step 9. String one of the larger beads.

Step 10. Follow the larger bead with another round bead.

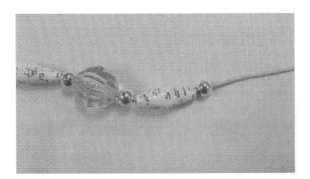

Step 11. Repeat the pattern (small round—fiction book bead—small round—larger bead—small round—fiction book bead—small round) until the desired length is met.

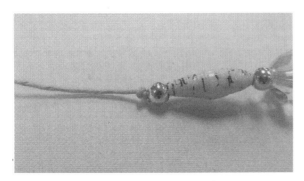

Step 12. Keeping to the pattern, end the necklace with a round bead. Tie a knot snug against the last bead without putting too much strain on the beads.

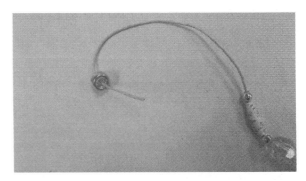

Step 13. String a pony bead through the end.

Step 14. Wrap the cording around the pony bead and tie the cord just above the existing knot. Double-knot it.

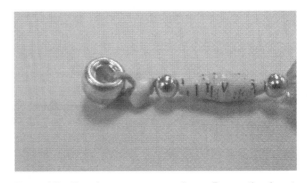

Step 15. Cut the excess cording. Cover the knot with craft glue to further secure the knot. Allow time to dry.

Step 16. Secure the necklace on the neck by pulling the pony bead through the hoop on the other end of the necklace.

Grow

Independent Challenge

Make an upcycled trinket, tassel, backpack or sports zipper pull, shoe bling, or jewelry from plastic bottles.

Equipment: conventional oven/toaster oven or heat gun, cookie pan, colored permanent markers, pliers, sturdy scissors

Supplies: recycled and cleaned plastic water bottles, twine, aluminum foil

Possible Supplies: coil-less safety pin, beading, string, jewelry bar pin, elastic cord, hemp cord, jewelry beads, pony beads

Learning and Building Knowledge

Craftster® Forum. "Making Beads from Plastic Bottles/" http://www.craftster.org/forum/index
   .php?topic=147089.0#axzz2NoI4AaYU
eHow™ money. "Plastic Bottle Making Process." http://www.ehow.com/how-does_5249914
   _plastic-bottle-making-process.html
New Zealand Institute of Chemistry. "Plastics Recycling." http://nzic.org.nz/ChemProcesses
   /environment
nikebetterworld. "Nike Better World - The Making of Nike Football National Team Jerseys."
   (video) http://www.youtube.com/watch?v=wEKFJWdJ5jg
Spoonful. "Make Plastic Beads." http://spoonful.com/crafts/make-plastic-beads

Share

Make step-by-step instructional materials for others to follow on how to repeat a custom design.

SOAPS AND SCRUBS

A lot of hand work is done in a makerspace. This can make for dirty, grubby hands needing a good scrubbing. Used coffee grounds are an excellent, natural body exfoliants, and effective scrub for removing strong odors from hands. Making traditional lye soap can be quite dangerous, but with a few modern conveniences, like a prepackaged soap base and microwave, no lye will be needed, therefore reducing the danger.

For the independent challenge, it might be appropriate to have the common ingredient on hand, but have the maker bring the more personal or expensive selections. If creating a body scrub, carefully research and adhere to the recommended packaging, storage, and shelf life guidelines.

Think

Learning and Building Knowledge

- Ground to Ground. "Coffee Grounds Make an Excellent Exfoliant!" http://groundtoground.org /2012/07/18/coffee-grounds-make-an-excellent-exfoliant
- Mayo Foundation for Medical Education and Research. "Adult Health – Hand Washing Do's and Don'ts." http://www.mayoclinic.com/health/hand-washing/HQ00407
- Starbucks Foodservice. "Starbucks Coffee Growing, Processing and Roasting." (video) http://www.youtube.com/watch?v=bNcx_E1x3D0

Create

Equipment: grater, microwave, microwave safe container, ½ cup measuring cup, measuring spoons, old muffin tin

Supplies: recycled paper, plastic wrap, used and dried coffee grounds, glycerin soap base, wood craft stick

Optional Materials: vanilla extract

Step 1. Line muffin tin with plastic wrap.

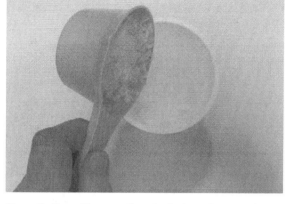

Step 4. Pour ½ cup of grated glycerin soap base into a microwave-safe container.

Step 5. Microwave on low, stopping frequently to stir with a wood craft stick. Stop microwaving once glycerin is nearly all melted. Do not overcook or boil.

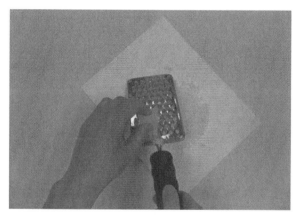

Step 2. Grate glycerin soap base onto a sheet of recycled paper.

Step 3. Lift the paper, turning it into a funnel, pouring the shavings into a measuring cup to equal ½ cup.

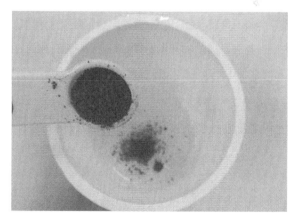

Step 6. Continuously stir. Add ½ teaspoon of used coffee grounds. While stirring, the soap will begin to turn brown. Don't add too much coffee, but, if while stirring it seems to need more, add a little bit at a time, but no more than ½ teaspoon more of coffee.

Step 7. Optional: Continue stirring and add ¼ teaspoon of vanilla extract.

Step 10. Once hardened, grab the corners of the plastic wrap to lift the soap from the mold.

Step 8. Stir until well mixed and glycerin thickens, but can still pour. This is tricky. If it isn't stirred, a film will develop on the top. If it gets too thick, it will clump. If it is too thin, the coffee grounds will sink to the bottom as it hardens in the mold. If it gets too thick, place it in the microwave for a few seconds and begin the process of stirring and thickening again.

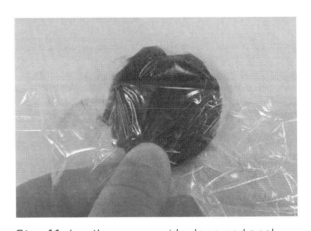

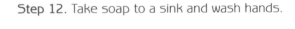

Step 11. Lay the soap upside down and peel back the plastic wrap. The maker should see coffee grounds interspersed throughout.

Step 12. Take soap to a sink and wash hands.

Step 9. Pour into plastic wrap–covered muffin tin to mold and leave soap to harden.

Grow

Independent Challenge

Make a soap by adding scents, colors, exfoliants, or decorative pieces, like flower petal and leaves, to make a personal soap or make an exfoliating body scrub with natural ingredients. Be imaginative and recycle from old containers or packaging from home. Have the maker bring in his own mold shape.

Equipment: grater, microwave, microwave-safe container, measuring cups, measuring spoons

Supplies: recycled paper, wax paper, used and dried coffee grounds, glycerin soap base, wood craft stick

Ingredient Possibilities: flower petals, used coffee grounds, oatmeal, cornmeal, essential oils or extracts, spices, beeswax, shea butter, cocoa butter, honey, loose tea, spices, cocoa powder, food coloring

Student Provides: recycled container to use as a mold, personal ingredients

Learning and Building Knowledge

Discovery Fit & Health. "How to Exfoliate Skin." http://health.howstuffworks.com/skin-care /cleansing/tips/how-to-exfoliate-skin1.htm

Homemade Gifts Made Easy. "Homemade Body Scrub." http://www.homemade-gifts-made -easy.com/homemade-body-scrub.html

McDaniel, Robert S. and Katherine J. McDaniel. *Soap Maker's Workshop: The Art and Craft of Natural Homemade Soap.* Krause Publications, 2010.

Tipnut. "18 Homemade Sugar, Sea Salt & Oatmeal Scrub Recipes." http://tipnut.com /homemade-sugar-scrub-recipes

Share

Create a recipe book, complete with pictures and step-by-step instructions, of successful custom soaps and scrubs.

TILE ART

My neighbor, Debbie Lloyd, is so creative and artistic. She can see an object and immediately think of what she could make from it. What talent. Recently, she had on display tiles decorated with family photos. Looking and looking at her creation, I was inspired to use her concept to create coasters with weeded fiction pages and illustrations from non-fiction, fiction, graphic novels, or picture books.

The illustration will be the centerpiece of the coaster, so select carefully. The image should be smaller than the coaster, but if it is not, try using just a portion or laying the picture at an angle to fit or trim the edges of the image until it is a good fit.

If planning to use the tile as an actual coaster, and not just decoration, be sure to finish the project with multiple coats of polyurethane or other moisture protection sealant.

Think

Learning and Building Knowledge

- CeratecChannel. "Ceramic tiles manufacturing process by Ceratec - How it's made?" (video) http://www.youtube.com/watch?v=-6UHfRXLwGI&feature=player_embedded
- TCNA Ceramic Tile News. "The History of Ceramic Tile in the United States." http://www.tileusa.com/historysp.htm
- The Tile Doctor®. "History of Tile." http://www.thetiledoctor.com/Tile-History

Create

Equipment: scissors, pencil, decorative scissors, sponge brush
Supplies: newsprint, weeded illustrated book, weeded fiction book, 4 x 4 inch bathroom tile, Mod Podge®, polyurethane spray, adhesive backed felt
Optional Materials: sandpaper, rocks

Guided Exploratory Experience

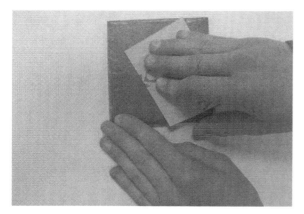

Step 1. Optional: Prep the tile by sanding and washing it. Set aside to dry.

Step 2. Look through weeded book illustrations to select an image ½ inch smaller than the tile and tear out the page. For example, if the tile is 4 × 4 inches, then the image should be no more than 3½ × 3½ inches.

Step 3. Use scissors to cut out the shape. Trim as necessary to enhance the design and comfortably fit inside the tile.

Step 4. Tear a page out of the center of a weeded fiction book.

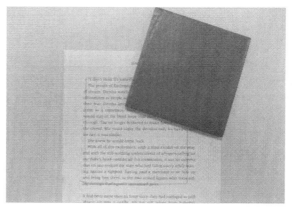

Step 5. Lay the tile on top of the text. Trace the tile outline onto the page.

Step 6. Select a pair of decorative scissors and cut *inside* the lines. Try to cut as straight as possible.

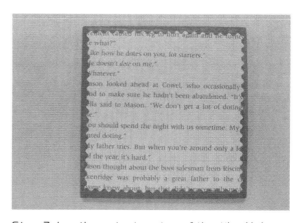

Step 7. Lay the cutout on top of the tile. Make sure the edges of the tile can still be seen and the edges are straight. Trim as needed, or start over with a new page if necessary. This will be the picture mat.

Step 8. Lay newsprint down to protect the work surface. With a sponge brush, coat the tile surface with Mod Podge®.

Step 12. Place the image on top of the mat while it is still wet and tacky. Smooth it out to work out any bubbles. Wait until thoroughly dry.

Step 13. Optional: If illustration was done in pieces that need layered, repeat Steps 11 and 12 as needed.

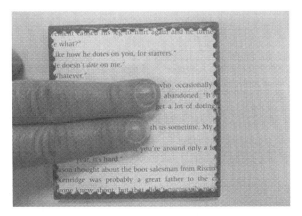

Step 9. Place the fiction mat carefully on top of the glue so that it is centered. Quickly work out any bubbles, smoothing down the surface with two fingers.

Step 10. Wait fifteen minutes. Allowing time to dry reduces the risk of the next layer wrinkling.

Step 14. Once dry, use the sponge brush to Mod Podge® over the top of the coaster. Wipe any excess off the side with a finger. Allow at least thirty minutes to dry.

Step 11. After waiting fifteen minutes, use the sponge brush to brush a coat of Mod Podge® over the top of the coaster.

Step 15. Brush a second coat over the top, brushing in the opposite direction.

Step 16. Once dry, take the coaster, newsprint, and polyurethane spray can outside.

Step 17. Lay down the newsprint to protect the ground. Place rocks on the corners of the newsprint to hold it in place. Put the coaster in the center of the newsprint.

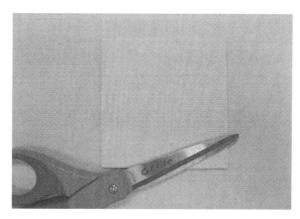

Step 20. Cut out the felt square.

Step 18. Follow the instructions on the can to spray a thin coat on the coaster. Allow time to dry and repeat as directed in the instructions on the can.

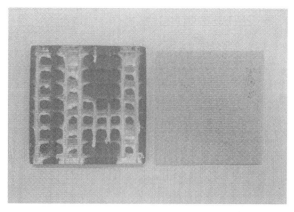

Step 21. Turn the tile upside down. Trim the felt square as needed to ensure the felt does not hang over the tile.

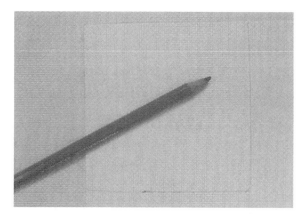

Step 19. Turn the felt upside down so the adhesive back is facing up. Lay the tile in the corner and trace around the tile.

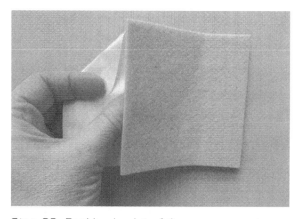

Step 22. Peel back a bit of the paper covering the adhesive. Carefully lay the adhesive side of the felt on the tile.

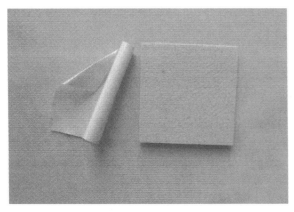

Step 23. Once the first edge is safely adhered, pull the rest of the paper off and secure the felt base to the back of the tile.

Step 25. The coaster is now ready for use.

Step 24. Turn the tile over and make sure no pieces of the felt base are showing. If they are, take scissors and carefully trim off the exposed edges.

Grow

Independent Challenge

Create a trivet by building a collage with images and words from weeded books and arranging them on a recycled floor tile. Because this is utilizing a recycled floor tile, be sure to use steel wool or other abrasive to scrub any residual dirt, grime, and grout from the front, back, and sides of the tile.

Equipment: scissors, pencil, decorative scissors, sponge brush

Supplies: newsprint, weeded illustrated books, weeded fiction book, used floor tile, Mod Podge®, polyurethane spray, adhesive backed felt, sandpaper, steel wool

Learning and Building Knowledge

Merriam-Webster. "Trivet." http://www.merriam-webster.com/dictionary/trivet

Sekora, John J. "Ceramic Tile in 20th Century America." Jersey Shore Publications, 2003.

The Tile Doctor®. "Tile Factory Tour." http://www.thetiledoctor.com/Tile-Factory

Share

Host an art show to display the tiles, or enter the tiles in a local or regional art fair.

VIDEO PRODUCTION

Young producers, directors, actors, and writers have an incredible array of venues today for self publication of video productions, including the currently trending YouTube, personal websites, virtual contests, and social networking sites. My own son, Trevor Preddy, a high school sophomore, has been involved in many of his friends' productions, including those published on YouTube, accepted and aired on the school's student televised news station, and entered electronically to win local and national awards.

Video production is now available to the general public through intuitive, simplified digital editing systems, which can be free and inexpensive online and desktop applications. Many students have video recording and still photo devices on their phones. All of which makes making a movie much easier and accessible.

Video can be created through video slideshows, like the currently popular and free for educators Microsoft Photo Story or Animoto. These incorporate images, text, and music to convey information and meaning. A video slideshow is a way to toy with video production as makers dabble with, in a very simplified way, script, storyboard, mood, and tone. For example, in the guided exploratory experience, get comfortable and gain basic experience by creating a book commercial.

Once confidence is gained, makers are ready for the independent challenge of creating a video utilizing a detailed script with storyboard and incorporating images, videos, music, narration, and transitions.

Think

Learning and Building Knowledge

- For Dummies®. "Storyboarding Your Film." http://www.dummies.com/how-to/content/story boarding-your-film.html
- Garrison, Andew. "Video Basics and Production Projects for the Classroom." Center for Media Literacy. http://www.medialit.org/reading-room/video-basics-and-production-projects-classroom
- Movie Outline. "A Glossary of Screenwriting Terms & Filmmaking Definitions." http://www.movie outline.com/articles/a-glossary-of-screenwriting-terms-and-filmmaking-definitions.html

Create

Equipment: computer, Internet, microphone, digital camera, video camera, tripod
Supplies: props, costumes, storyboard materials, sticky notes
Video Slideshow Program: one already used and authorized by the school district or other possibilities include: Animoto http://animoto.com/education, Microsoft Photo Story 3 http://www.microsoft.com /en-us/download/default.aspx

CREDITS
Do the Right Thing:
Give Credit for Image, Audio, and Video Use

When you copy and paste a picture from someone's website, and you haven't taken the picture, you must cite it to avoid plagiarism. To do this:

1. Create a word document and save it to your drive in your project's folder so you can find it later. Save it as "Credits" and your last name.
2. To save
   - PICTURES & IMAGES
     - Right Click on the picture and do a Save As...
     - Save it to your drive in your project folder so you can use it later.
     - When saving, name the file a one or two word description of what it is, like "baseball game."
   - MUSIC & SOUND EFFECTS
     - Search for the sound needed to set the right mood and tone. Use the *Preview* option to listen.
     - To save, click on your selection. If given a choice of length, choose 60 since our commercials will be approximately 60 seconds long.
     - When the Save bar pops up, click the arrow next to Save and select Save As from the menu.
     - Save it to your drive in your project folder so you can use it later.
3. Open your Credits word document.
   1. List the name of the image.
   2. Right Click on the web address and click Copy, then right click and Paste the URL address under the image name so you can use it later.

Solid Background Colors
These are special websites with solid color: .gif/.jpg images to download for background. A solid background is helpful for titles and credits.

- Windows Photo Story: Adding a Title-Only Slide - http://www.windowsphotostory.com/guides/titleslides/adding-a-tile-only-slide.aspx
- Solid Color Blocks - http://hs.nazarethasd.k12.pa.us/Solid%20Color%20Blocks/area.htm

Clip Art for School Projects
Special websites with copyright free, Creative Commons, or educational rights to use for assignment.

- Creative Commons – http://search.creativecommons.org/
  Rights are given to use some works found through Creative Commons. Once the website for the items is opened, follow the license link on the page for that item to investigate the use rights, which could be the CC logo or the words, copyright, rights, permission, etc. If in doubt, do not use
- Open Clip Art - http://openclipart.org/browse
- School Clip Art - http://www.school-clip-art.com/

Pictures for School Projects
Special websites with copyright free, Creative Commons, or educational rights to use for assignment.

- Arkive – http://www.arkive.org/
  Images and video of animals. Education rights are "for internal private educational use by educators and students (for example they may be used in lessons, presentations, school projects etc)." So, use it for a project, but don't publish it on the web or distribute it in any other way.
- Creative Commons – http://search.creativecommons.org/
  Rights are given to use some works found through Creative Commons. Once the website for the items is opened, follow the license link on the page for that item to investigate the use rights, which could be the CC logo or the words, copyright, rights, or permission. If in doubt, do not use.
- Edupic - http://edupic.net/

CREDITS

Do the Right Thing:
Give Credit for Image, Audio, and Video Use

- Flickr - http://www.flickr.com/
  Once an image is found, look at the *license* for the sharing rights.
- Free Photo Bank - http://www.freephotobank.org/main.php
  Wikimedia Commons - http://commons.wikimedia.org/wiki/Main_Page
- Ookaboo - http://ookaboo.com/o/pictures/
- Pics4Learning - http://pics4learning.com/
- Getty Images - http://www.gettyimages.com/
  Select *Royalty Free* images, but there is still a fee to legally use, so do not use unless you pay.

Video for School Projects

Special websites with copyright free, Creative Commons, or educational rights to use for assignment.

- Wikimedia Commons - http://commons.wikimedia.org/wiki/Main_Page
  "A media file repository making available public domain and freely-licensed educational media content (images, sound and video clips) to everyone"
- Creative Commons – http://search.creativecommons.org/
  Rights are given to use some works found through Creative Commons. Once the website for the items is opened, follow the license link on the page for that item to investigate the use rights, which could be the CC logo or the words, copyright, rights, permission, etc. If in doubt, do not use
- Arkive – http://www.arkive.org/
  Images and video of animals. Education rights are "for internal private educational use by educators and students (for example they may be used in lessons, presentations, school projects etc)." So, use it for a project, but don't publish it on the web or distribute it in any other way.

Music for School Projects

Special websites with copyright free, Creative Commons, or educational rights to use for assignment.

- Bargus Music Library - http://www.bargus.org/musiclibrary.html
- ccMixter Music Discovery - http://dig.ccmixter.org/
  After doing a search, click on the CC logo next to the song title for the use rights of that particular sound. (Click on the " Instrumental Music for Film, YouTube™ Videos and Soundtracks" link for music without vocals.)
- Jewelbeat - http://www.jewelbeat.com/
  Per song download cost is currently comparable to any music download. Rights are not for an individual, not for multiple users. So it can't be shared, distributed or used by friends, a class, a school, etc.)
- Royalty Free Music - http://www.royaltyfreemusic.com/free-music-clips.html
  "RoyaltyFreeMusic.com offers a diverse set of free royalty free music clips that can be used, without limitation, in educational, student and personal, not-for-profit projects, free of charge… must cite Royalty Free Music.com, as the source of the music and - when possible- provide a link to our site."

Sound Effects for School Projects

Special websites with copyright free, Creative Commons, or educational rights to use for assignment.

- Bargus Sound Library – http://www.bargus.org/soundlibrary.html
- Flash Kit – http://www.flashkit.com/soundfx/
- Free Sound Effects - http://www.stonewashed.net/sfx.html
- Media College Free Sound Effects - http://www.mediacollege.com/downloads/sound-effects/
- PacDV free sound effects - http://www.pacdv.com/sounds/index.html
- Sound Jay - http://www.soundjay.com/
- Soundgator - http://www.soundgator.com/

Guided Exploratory Experience

Step 1. Begin creating a video slideshow book commercial by reading the chosen book.

Step 2. While reading, flag pages with sticky notes with script ideas. This includes writing brief quotes from the book, character relationships and characteristics, major plot developments, and ideas for symbolic images.

Step 3. Prepare a script and storyboard intended to capture the interest of the viewer, enticing viewers to want what the creator is promoting— the book. Include in the storyboard a title slide and credits slide.

Book Commercial
Slideshow Storyboard

Book Title: _____

Author: _____ Copyright date: _____

Setting: _____ Genre: _____

Mood: _____

Other Important Ideas and Notes:

1   Your task is to develop a storyboard to help organize your thoughts just as you would if you were producer developing a music video, television program, or movie.
2   Prepare to create your commercial using no more than 15 slides.
3   Every book commercial will start with a title and book cover.
4   Every book commercial will end with the book cover and credits.
5   Draw an 'X' through any box on the storyboard not needed.

Background/Theme Music Ideas: _____

1	2	3 Text to place on top of the color or image:
Title: Author: Background Color:	COVER of BOOK	List of Ideas for a Solid Color Background or Symbolic Images:

4 Text to place on top of the
color or image:

List of Ideas for a
Solid Color Background or
Symbolic Images:

5 Text to place on top of the
color or image:

List of Ideas for a
Solid Color Background or
Symbolic Images:

6 Text to place on top of the
color or image:

List of Ideas for a
Solid Color Background or
Symbolic Images:

7 Text to place on top of the
color or image:

List of Ideas for a
Solid Color Background or
Symbolic Images:

8 Text to place on top of the
color or image:

List of Ideas for a
Solid Color Background or
Symbolic Images:

9 Text to place on top of the
color or image:

List of Ideas for a
Solid Color Background or
Symbolic Images:

10 Text to place on top of the
color or image:

List of Ideas for a
Solid Color Background or
Symbolic Images:

11

COVER
of
BOOK

12

IMAGE SOURCES:

Step 4. Take or locate needed pictures according to the storyboard and script.

Step 5. Review the training materials available for the selected video editing system.

Step 6. Use the video editing slideshow program to create a video incorporating motion, images, text, and copyright compliant music.

CREATING A VIDEO SLIDESHOW BOOK COMMERCIAL
Photo Story 3 for Windows

ALWAYS REMEMBER:
1. Use the sticky notes to flag pages and write down ideas for the commercial while reading.
2. Once the reading is complete, use the sticky notes as inspiration for completing the storyboard.
3. After the Storyboard is drafted, follow the instructions on the Credits handout to create a folder, save items to the folder and document credits for using those items in the project.
4. Remember to frequently save while working on the Photo Story.

Starting the Project
- Open Photo Story.
- Choose to 'Begin a Story' or, if returning to complete a project, choose 'Edit a Project.'
- Then click Next.

Import Selected Images
- Click Import Pictures and locate the folder where your images are saved.
- Add images one at a time or add the whole group by clicking on the first image then hold the Ctrl (control) key down and use your mouse to click and select the rest of the images, then click Ok.

Organize Images
- Click and drag images until they are in the correct order on the timeline.
- Click Save. Save the project in the same folder created for the images and credits document.

Crop an Image (if needed)
Crop an image if there are black edges around the picture on the time you wish to remove or if only a portion of the image needed or wanted
- If an image on the timeline needs to be cropped (remove part of the image), right click on the image on the timeline. From the box that opens up, click on Edit, then on Crop.
- Make sure the checkmark is in the Crop box.
- Use the mouse to drag the crop box around.
- Use the corners to click and drag the crop box to make it larger or smaller (remember: the smaller the image is cropped, the poorer the image might become in the final product)
- Use the arrows to select other images and repeat the process for all images requiring a crop.
- Save the changes and close the edit box.
- **Once done, click the Next button below the Timeline to continue to the next step.**

Add Text

- Click on the slide in the timeline so it appears in the large preview box.
- Type the text from your Storyboard into the text box.
- Use the icons above the text box to change the text placement, size, color, and font design.
- Arrange the text in an artful manner which helps emphasize the mood and meaning behind them.

CREATING A VIDEO SLIDESHOW BOOK COMMERCIAL
Photo Story 3 for Windows

Add an Effect
- Once the text has been placed, an effect may be needed.
- Especially effective for reducing the harshness of an image and bringing the text forward is *Washout.*
- Remember:
  - Some slides may not need any effect.
  - Using too many different effects can harm the overall look of the final product.

- **Once done, click the Next button below the Timeline to continue to the next step.**

- **Click on Customize Motion below the preview screen.**

Add Motion
This is optional and not required of every slide. Each slide is unique and some slides are more powerful without the distraction of motion. For slides with motion:
- Start with the first slide in the timeline requiring motion.
- Check the box that says *Specify start and end position of motion.*
  - *Start position* is the box on the left. Use the mouse to change the size and location of the box. For example, place it around the text, or even just the most important words of the text.
  - *End position* is the box on the right. Use the mouse to make the End Position in the right box the full screen.
  - Be creative. Use the motion Start and End positions to help emphasize the text.
- Click the arrow button to move to the next slide until all slides requiring motion have been done.

Add Transition
This is optional and not required of every slide. Each slide is unique and some slides are more powerful without the distraction of a transition. For slides with motion:
- Click on the Transition tab.
- Start with the first slide in the timeline requiring a transition.
- A preview of the transition will appear in the center box.
- Scroll through the Transitions for the best choice the image and meaning of the two slides. Click on the Transition icon for a sneak peek.
- Once the right fit is found, click on the Transition icon to select.
- Click the arrow button move to the next slide until all slides requiring Transitions have been done. Click Save.
- Go back to the beginning slide and click Preview to be sure everything looks its best.Close the preview box.
- Click Close to close the Customize Motion box.

Narrate Your Picture and Customize Motion
- The Book Commercial will not be narrated, so click the *Next* button below the Timeline to skip this step and go to the **Add Background Music** screen.

CREATING A VIDEO SLIDESHOW BOOK COMMERCIAL
Photo Story 3 for Windows

Add Background/Theme Music
- Plug in headphones or earbuds and put them on.
- Click on the *Create Music* button.

Another option is to use Royalty Free music selected for this project or a completely original work created, performed and recorded by you.

Create Music
- Once the Create Music box appears, use all the options available to select the right theme of music to match the genre and mood of the book.
    - Options include music genre, style, type of band, moods.
    - Then adjust the tempo (speed) and intensity.
- Click Play to preview the background music created.
- Click Ok to accept the music.
- With earbuds still on, click *Preview* to view the final project from beginning to end. Make note of any desired changes or problems. Go back and fix.
- Once everything is good, **click *Save Project* then *Next*.**

Save Your Story
This step is very important. Right now this is still a project, but the project needs to go through a process called rendering, which converts the project into a finalized, sharable format. The project will still exist for later revisions, if needed.
- Click the *Browse* button.
    - In the window that pops up, select location for your final video. Change the file name and click Save.
- Click the Settings button.
    - Under *Profile* in the pop-up window select **Profile for computers – 4**.
    - Click the I to close the window.
- Click Next to begin saving the movie. Wait patiently while it converts the project final into a playable format.

- **Once it is done, click the *View Your Story* button to preview the final video.**
  Make any corrections, if needed, and resave.

Congratulations! You have now created a book commercial.

Grow

Independent Challenge

Work with a team to write, plan, direct, act, record, edit, and produce a short film.

Equipment: computer, printer, video editing software, cloud computing, Internet, microphone, digital camera, video camera, tripod

Supplies: props, costumes, storyboard, script

Video Editing Program: One already used and authorized by the school district or research to find one to best fit the needs of the makerspace. For example, desktop editing with CyberLink's PowerDirector: http://www.cyberlink.com/products/powerdirector or cloud editing with WeVideo: https://www.wevideo.com/.

Learning and Building Knowledge

Jamendo. http://www.jamendo.com

Stanford University. "Tutorial-Video Production Basics: Shooting Better Video." (videos) http://acomp.stanford.edu/tutorials/video_production_basics

Video Production Tips. "Lighting Basics for Video Making." http://videoproductiontips.com/lighting-basics-for-video-making

WikiHow. "How to Edit Movies." http://www.wikihow.com/Edit-Movies

Share

1. Publish video slideshow book commercials during the school's televised news program.
2. Post videos on the school website.
3. Air videos through the school's in-house television system.
4. Enter productions into local, state or national competitions.

YARN MÂCHÉ

Yarn has become such an intriguing textile. The range of colors, weights, and textures is nearly limitless. Use repurposed yarn to make a bookmark, ornament, window, or wall decoration for the guided activity, then a more advanced independent project of a bowl.

Yarn can be repurposed from outgrown, outworn, or unfashionable clothing and scarves. The items can be washed, dried, then the yarn unraveled. Items can be unraveled at point of need, or taken apart in advance, rolled back into balls, and stored until needed for larger projects. Yarn may then also be upcycled for knitting, crochet, fine arts, and crafts.

Think

 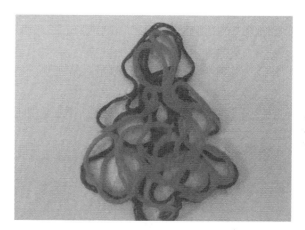

Learning and Building Knowledge

- About.com Knitting. "Recycling Yarn From a Knit Sweater." http://knitting.about.com/od/toolsand supplies/ss/recycling-yarn.htm
- Cyberseams. "How to Braid Hair." (video) http://www.youtube.com/watch?v=F_hHhtQGNus &feature=player_embedded#!
- How Products are Made Volume 3. "Yarn." http://www.madehow.com/Volume-3/Yarn.html
- Smithsonian National Museum of American History Behring Center. "History-What is Paper Mâché." http://americanhistory.si.edu/anatomy/history/nma03_history_whatis.html
- Wool and Yarn. "A History of Yarn." http://www.woolandyarn.co.uk/a-history-of-yarn-c147.html

Create

Equipment: cookie cutter

Supplies: old sweaters and scarves, yarn mâché paste (see recipe on page 118), parchment paper, wood craft stick

Optional Materials: needle with eye large enough for yarn, disposable gloves

Yarn Mâché Paste

Ingredients:
- o Liquid Fabric Stiffener
- o Glue (white, any brand)
- o Water

Supplies:
- o Recycled plastic or glass container with lid
- o Measuring cups and spoons
- o Small rubber spatula

Mix 2/3 glue to 1/3 fabric stiffener. Paste should be thick enough that it does not drip or run, but thin enough to be absorbed by the yarn. If it is too thick, carefully add water, one teaspoon at a time, until correct consistency. Cover until needed. Stir before use.

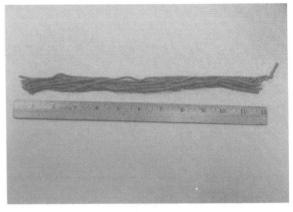

Step 2. Unravel sweaters and scarves until it looks like enough yarn to fill a thin layer in the cookie cutter shape. Cut into manageable lengths, about 9–15 inches each. Unravel and cut three extra pieces of yarn, 2 feet long each, and set aside.

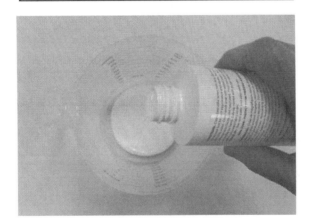

Step 3. Select a cookie cutter shape and cut out a square of parchment paper a few inches larger than the shape. Place the cookie cutter on the parchment paper.

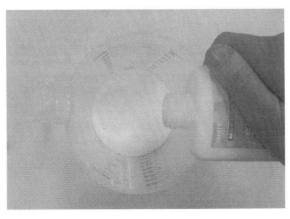

Step 1. Make yarn mâché paste.

Step 4. Stir yarn mâché paste with a wood craft stick.

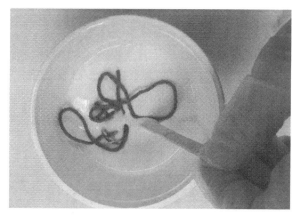

Step 5. Dip a few cut lengths of yarn and push down into the paste with the craft stick to soak.

Step 8. Lay yarn in random squiggles throughout the shape. Continue Steps 4–7 until the shape has a thin layer.

Step 6. If using disposable gloves, put them on now. As one length of yarn is being taken out of the glue, pinch the yarn between two fingers and pull it through to squeeze off the excess glue.

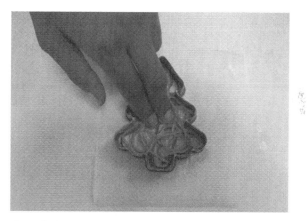

Step 9. Wash and dry hands, or remove gloves, then press the yarn flat with the front and back of fingertips. Make sure all yarn is pressed together so that it will dry into one form.

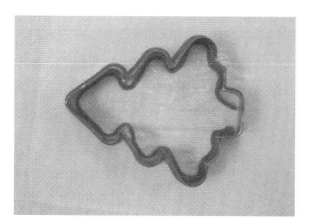

Step 7. Lay yarn inside the edges to outline the shape.

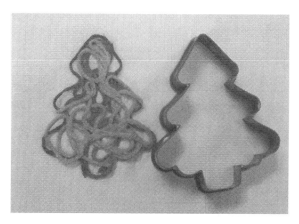

Step 10. Wait ten minutes, then gently lift the cookie cutter off, leaving the yarn shape on the parchment. Allow to dry completely, approximately twenty-four hours.

Step 11. Once dry, take the three pieces of 2 foot yarn and thread through one edge of shape. For strength, it might be helpful to thread through three separate, yet nearby, holes. Use a yarn needle if unable to do this by hand.

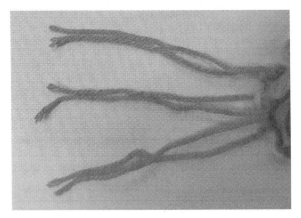

Step 12. Pull each piece through to even out the ends so that there are six equal lengths.

Step 14a. To make a bookmark, knot the end.

Step 13. Separate each double strand so that there are three groups and braid as if braiding hair.

Step 14b. To hang as a window or wall decoration or holiday ornament, make a loop of the braid and knot at the base.

Step 15. If desired, cut off loose ends.

Grow

Independent Challenge

Consider the artistic placement of colors and designs to create a yarn mâché bowl for tabletop decoration and strong enough to hold contents.

For the independent challenge, makers will use a blown-up balloon, as is often used in traditional paper mâché projects. A problem to be solved is how to create a flat base for the bowl. With a little thought, this can be solved with a circle of cardstock, leveled, then taped to the bottom of the balloon, which will become the base of the bowl. Another consideration is how much tape to lay between the cardstock and balloon to secure it in place, as well as provide a solid surface for which the yarn to adhere. To keep the cardstock and tape from inappropriately sticking to the final product, wrap the bowl-shaped balloon with plastic wrap. This will ensure the project will easily pull away once the yarn is dry. The final consideration is to wrap the pasted yarn onto the base of the bowl in a single layer, circular fashion so that the final bowl's base remains flat and stable.

Equipment: circle punch, small level

Supplies: repurposed yarn, yarn mâché paste, card stock, tape, balloon, newsprint, plastic wrap

Optional: disposable gloves

Learning and Building Knowledge

Interweave Craft. "Knitting Dailt TV Yarn Spotlight: Episode 1001 - Made in America" (video)
    https://www.youtube.com/watch?v=PYN5w5HR6Vs
National Geographic Green Living. "How to Reuse or Recycle Apparel and Textiles. http://green
    living.nationalgeographic.com/reuse-recycle-apparel-textiles-2927.html

Share

Coordinate with a local non-profit, senior home, or philanthropic organization to make yarn mâché ornaments and place them on the organization's holiday tree.

Make and Take

Sometimes simple is needed. There are occasions when the makerspace needs a quick and easy self-directed activity which can be done in one efficient visit, or as part of a come-when-you-can group task.

An important point to consider is the full range of patronage. It is important to keep in mind that not all of the students serviced in the school library are interested in in-depth or lengthy tasks. Those students may be attracted to the makerspace, but turned off by the commitment required for the more complicated tasks. Simple activities may draw larger crowds who are intimidated by those more technical projects. Some of the patronage may only want to get involved in these simple events, so hosting these smaller happenings fills an important niche. These simple events are also an opportunity to allow those intimidated patrons to grow comfortable with the make concept and draw them toward participating in

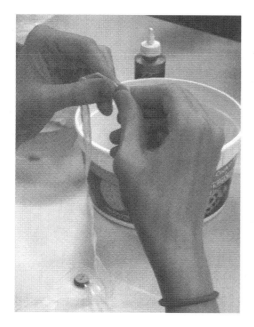

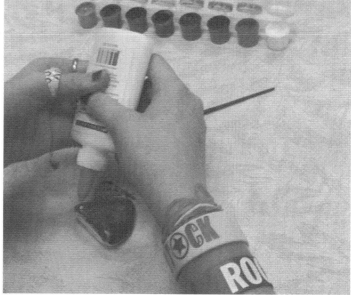

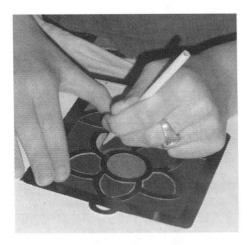

some of the deeper makerspace events which coincide with their personal interests.

Simple projects are also a transitional activity. Often, bigger projects require a bit of time and organization to set up. A simple activity can be set up quickly to keep the makerspace active while the makerspace coordinator prepares and stages the next, deeper-learning, skills-embedded project.

Simple projects can also be training ground for navigating group dynamics. This is an opportunity for students to practice teamwork without being committed to a complicated, lengthy, group make.

- Education.com. "Science Activities and Experiments." http://www.education.com /activity/science
- LeBaron, Marie. *Make and Takes for Kids: 50 Crafts Throughout the Year*. Wiley, 2011.
- Make and Takes™. http://www.makeandtakes.com
- Morgan, Richela Fabian. *Tape It & Make It: 101 Duct Tape Activities*. Barron's Educational Series, Inc., 2012.
- NASA. "Make and Take Activities." http://www.nasa.gov/topics/solarsystem/sunearth system/main/PO_makeAndTake.html

Bookmarks

Bookmarks are always an affordable library make and take. They're easily done in one visit, can be thrown together with random odds-and-ends supplies, and are relatable. To make it even more affordable, use recycled and donated materials. Don't want bookmarks? Make some modifications and convert the activity to a magnet, bulletin board decoration, door hanging, or holiday ornament.

Button Bookmark

Equipment: scissors, ruler
Supplies: ribbon, glue dots, buttons, tape

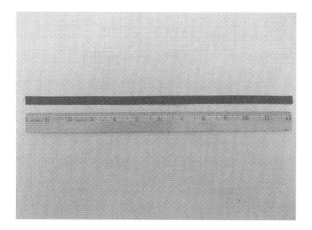

Step 1. Select a ribbon and cut a 12 inch strip.

Step 2. Select four buttons as fat as, or fatter than, the glue dots.

Step 3. Place a glue dot on one end of the ribbon.

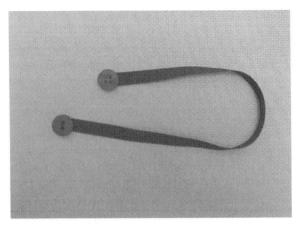

Step 5. Repeat Steps 3 and 4 on the opposite end of the ribbon.

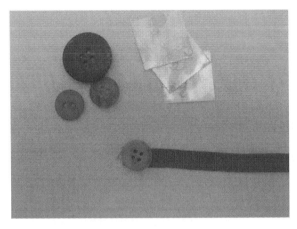

Step 4. Press a button, flat side down, onto the glue dot.

Step 6. Turn the ribbon over. Repeat Steps 3 and 4 on both ends of the other side of the ribbon, centering the button on top of the preexisting button.

Paint Strip Bookmark

Equipment: thesaurus, dictionary, hole punch, craft punches smaller than the paint chip colors
Supplies: donated paint strips, colored permanent markers, curling ribbon, double-sided tape

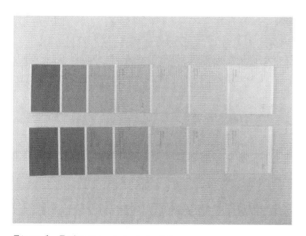

Step 1. Select two paint strips.

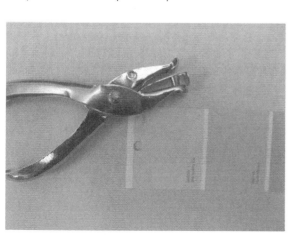

Step 2. Punch a hole in the top center of one paint strip.

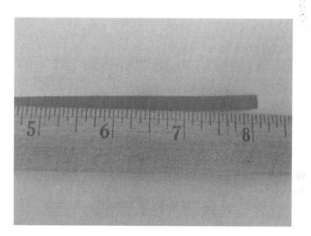

Step 3. Cut an 8 inch strip of curling ribbon.

Step 4. Fold the curling ribbon in half and push the loop through the hole in the paint strip.

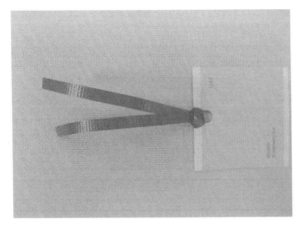

Step 5. Bring the two tails of the ribbon through the loop, then pull tight to make the bookmark ribbon.

Step 8. Select a permanent marker color and place one letter of the word in each shape.

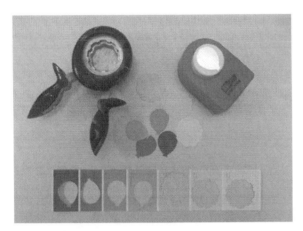

Step 6. Select a craft punch and punch a shape out of each color of the other paint strip. Count the number of shapes punched.

Step 7. Use the thesaurus and dictionary to select a motivational word. The word can have no more letters in it than the number of shapes punched out.

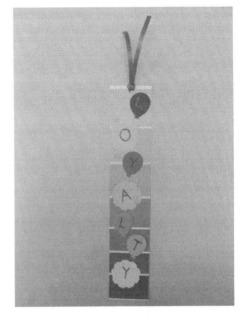

Step 9. Use double-sided tape to stick each letter, in order, on the bookmark, running top to bottom.

Pony Bead Bookmark

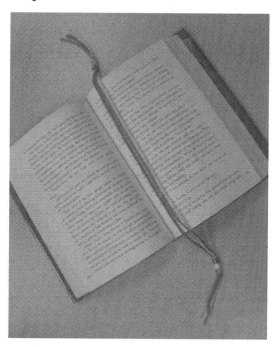

Equipment: scissors, ruler
Supplies: yarn, pony beads, office tape

Step 1. Choose up to three different yarns. Cut three pieces, 15–18 inches each.

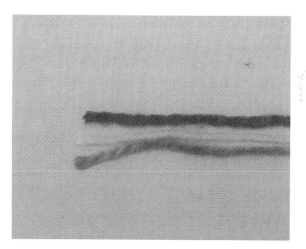

Step 2. Lay out the three lengths side by side so the ends are lined up together.

Step 3. Tie the three together with a knot about 2½ inches from the end.

Step 4. Repeat on the opposite end.

Step 5. Select six pony beads.

Step 6. Roll the yarn together with a piece of tape. Have the tape hanging over the yarn, roll the yarn and tape tightly onto the end of yarn, rolling the pieces together, then pinch the tape end. It should be small enough to fit through the hole of a pony bead.

Step 7. String three pony beads onto one end.

Step 8. Push the beads against the knot. Tie a knot tightly against the end of the pony beads to hold them in place. Tug off the tape.

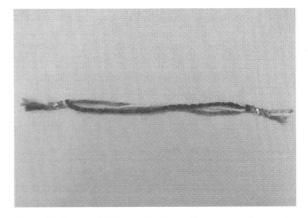

Step 9. Repeat Steps 6–8 on the opposite end.

Variation: After Step 3, braid the length of the yarn before tying a knot on the other end.

Desk Blotter

As my high school age son can attest, students still spend a lot of time at their desk completing homework, messing around on the computer, drawing, writing, and much more. Personalize that space by creating a desk blotter. Don't want a desk blotter? Use it for a kitchen placemat, project work surface, or turn it into a fine arts wall décor. If not enough weeded illustrated books and book jackets available, also use upcycled materials like used gift wrap, gift bags, and catalogs.

Equipment: scissors, laminator, box cutter
Supplies: spray adhesive, nine-by-twelve (or twelve-by-eighteen) inch construction paper, lamination film, newsprint, and weeded book jackets and book pages with graphics

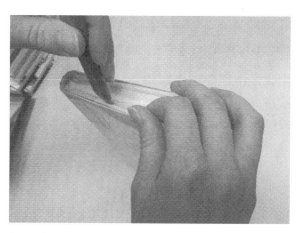

Step 1. Remove book jackets from weeded library books.

Step 2. Use scissors to carefully cut out around the outline of images from old book jackets and illustrations from weeded books. Cut out more than enough to make a layered art pattern on the construction paper.

Step 3. Among the scrap pieces, cut out rectangles and squares of solid colors for the border. Cut out more than enough for the border.

Step 4. Select a piece of construction paper for the mat.

Step 7. Use the trimmed images to make a design within the frame. Place larger pieces down first. Continue layering until satisfied.

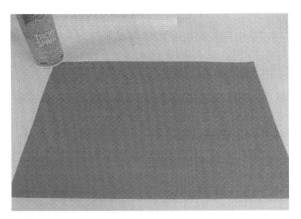

Step 5. Lay the construction paper on a work surface protected with newsprint. Follow the instructions on the spray can and coat the construction paper with a thin layer of spray adhesive.

Step 8. Laminate the project, then trim the lamination, leaving a ¼ inch of laminate around the perimeter of the paper.

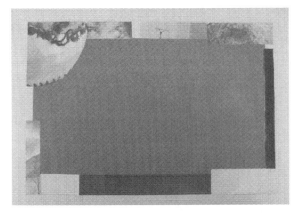

Step 6. Starting with the edges, use the rectangle and square scraps to make a border.

Desktop Write-on Board

It is often necessary to write notes for oneself or others, including to-do lists, reminders, quick how-to's, shopping lists, and much more. A reusable write-on board is environmentally thoughtful, especially when using repurposed materials, like an old picture frame. This craft was inspired by Sarah Belt, the Perry Meridian middle grades orchestra director who had a variation of this project in her workspace in a multitude of sizes and shapes. The idea was great, so I couldn't wait to try it out with a few modifications.

Equipment: scissors

Supplies: glass cleaner, paper towels or hand towel, newsprint, old tabletop picture frame, used gift wrap tissue paper (it can be wrinkled), pencil, spray adhesive, dry erase marker

Optional Materials: small alphabet stickers, used gift wrap cut into ribbon-like strips (allow students to cut the strips using decorative edge scissors), glue, ribbon, yarn, lace

Step 1. Lay a piece of newsprint down to protect the work surface. Choose a frame from the selection available. Take apart the frame.

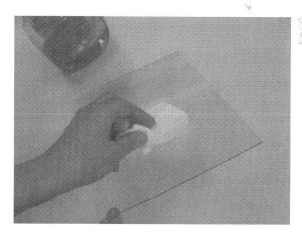

Step 2. Clean both sides of the glass and the frame. Set aside.

Step 3. Select a piece of gift wrap tissue paper. Lay it on the table, then place the frame backing upside down on the tissue paper. Use the pencil to trace approximately ½ to 1 inch outside the perimeter.

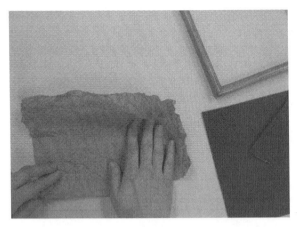

Step 4. Cut the tissue paper along the pencil lines. Wad the tissue into a ball in your palm, wrinkling the paper. Lay the tissue down on the workspace and flatten it out.

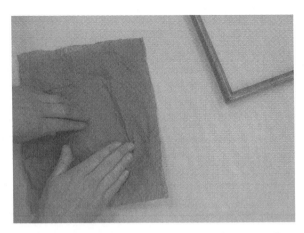

Step 6. Centering the tissue paper, lay it gently on the now tacky surface of the frame backing. Starting in the center and spanning outward, gently smooth out the tissue onto the backing. Note that the tissue will have a wrinkled appearance. Allow time to dry.

Step 5. Turn the frame backing over so the back is now on the workspace. Lightly spray the adhesive on the side of the frame backing which will face the glass.

Step 7. Optional: While the tissue paper is drying, select text or other decorative pieces to add to the border of the tissue covered frame backing, adding dimension and personalizing the frame. Be cautious. The more decorative pieces added, the less actual writing space available. As needed, carefully place glue on the back of prepared decorative pieces before strategically placing the items on the dry tissue paper. Allow time to dry.

Step 8. Carefully place glass back in the frame, then place the frame backing, decorated side down on top of the glass and re-attach to the frame.

Step 10. Stand up on table. Use dry erase marker on glass. Writing can be erased with wet tissue and replaced with new text at any time.

Step 9. Use scissors to trim away excess tissue paper or decorative pieces.

Journal Covers

• •

Young people never seem to be at a loss for writing their thoughts, dreams, experiences, theories, and so much more through narratives, poetry, journaling, and artwork. The only thing to make something so private even better is to personalize or disguise it.

Book Jacket Journal Cover

Equipment: scissors, ruler, weeded books

Supplies: composition notebook, pencil, weeded book jacket as tall or taller than the height of the composition notebook, newsprint, spray adhesive

Optional Materials: color permanent markers

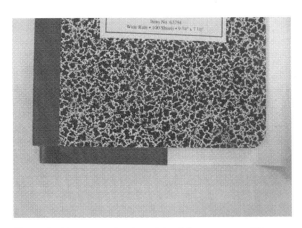

Step 1. Measure the height of the composition notebook. Open up the book jacket. Use the ruler to mark cutting lines off the top and bottom, as necessary to fit the height of the composition notebook, taking note of trim lines and how it will affect the aesthetics of the cover image.

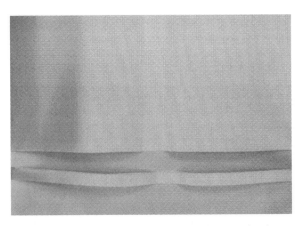

Step 2. Cut off the excess along the marked trim lines.

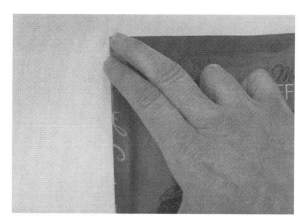

Step 3. Line up the corners and edges of the book jacket as perfectly as possible, then crease the center, or spine, with fingers and a ruler.

Step 6. Take the book jacket, open it on top of newsprint, then follow the direction on the spray adhesive to spray the inside of the book jacket.

Step 4. Place the composition notebook against the newly creased spine. Work the jacket along the length of the front of the notebook. Fold the excess over, just as one would for a book. Work a crease into the new flap fold.

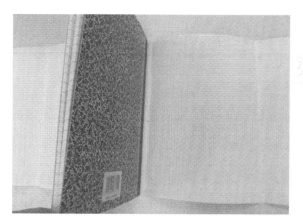

Step 7. Carefully place the composition notebook spine along the spine crease of the book jacket.

Step 5. Repeat Step 4 on the other flap.

Step 8. Continue to carefully lay the glued jacket onto the surface of the composition notebook. Continue to monitor the edges to make sure they line up.

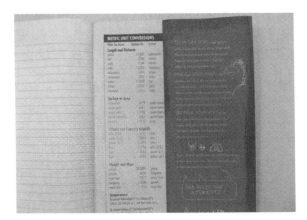

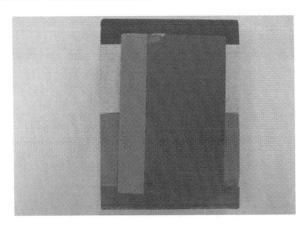

Step 9. Wrap the flaps around to the inside of the front and back cover.

Step 10. Optional: Personalize the jacket by adding to the artwork with the permanent marker colors.

Step 11. Place weeded books or other heavy object on top of the cover overnight.

Felt Journal Cover

Equipment: scissors, ruler, weeded books

Supplies: composition notebook, felt fabric, scraps of patterned felt fabric, felt sheets, glue, recycled paper

Optional Materials: craft jewels, self-adhesive foam letters

Step 1. Cut a 14 x 20 inch rectangle of solid felt fabric. This will be the composition notebook cover.

Step 2. Select and cut a 4½ x 5½ inch rectangle of patterned felt fabric. This will be the front pocket

Step 3. Cut two, 6 x 9 inch rectangles from the felt sheets. This will be for the inside of the cover.

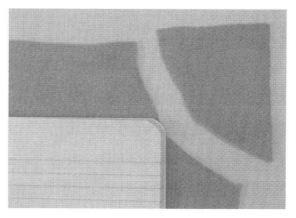

Step 4. Open the composition notebook and center it on the large, solid felt piece. Cut a notch out of each corner.

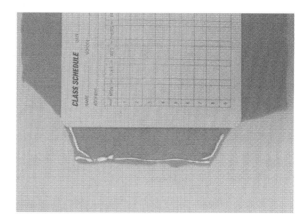

Step 5. Lay glue along the edges of the inside of the left flap of felt. Do not over-glue.

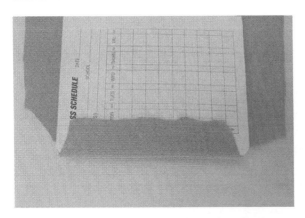

Step 6. Fold the flap over and snugly adhere to the inside cover of the composition notebook.

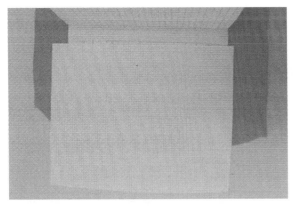

Step 7. Place a piece of recycled paper over the newly glued area and close the notebook.

Step 8. Open the back cover and repeat steps five through seven.

Step 9. On each end of the spine, trim a triangle of felt, ending at a point on the spine.

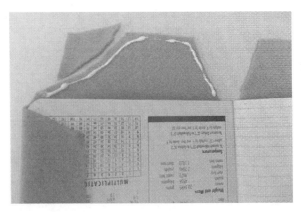

Step 10. Open to the front cover. Fold down the top flap of felt. Trim off any extra felt to ensure the felt lies flat and does not overlap. Repeat the process for the bottom flap.

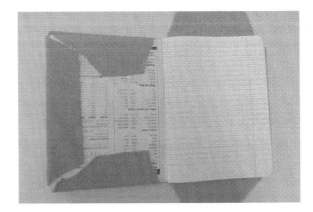

Step 11. Glue along the edges of the top flap and fold it over to snugly adhere to the inside cover of the composition notebook. Do not over-glue. Repeat for the bottom flap. Place a piece of recycled paper over the recently glued inside cover.

Step 12. Repeat Steps 10 and 11 for the inside of the back cover.

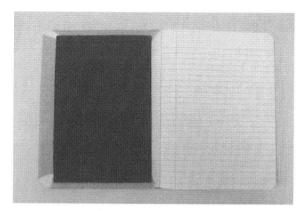

Step 13. Select one of the felt rectangles, lay a line of glue around the perimeter of the back. Turn it over and center it over the inside front cover. Press down to help the glue adhere. Repeat with the second rectangle for the inside of the back cover. Do not over-glue.

Step 16. Insert a sheet of recycled paper inside the back cover, inside the front cover, and over the pocket.

Step 14. To glue on the pocket, place a line of glue only along the sides and bottom of the back. Do not over-glue.

Step 17. Place a stack of weeded books as weight on the closed journal for a few hours or until glue is dry.

Step 15. Place the pocket in the desired location on the cover.

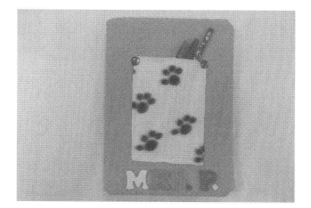

Step 18. Optional: Add craft jewels to the corners of the pocket. Place initials on the cover in foam letters.

Gift Wrap Photo Frame Journal Cover

Equipment: ruler, scissors, weeded books, paper trimmer

Supplies: composition notebook, gift wrap paper, newsprint, clear plastic pocket sized to fit a photograph, adhesive spray

Student Provides: photograph or artwork to fit inside the clear plastic pocket

Step 1. Cut a piece of gift wrap paper, 9¾ x 29 inches.

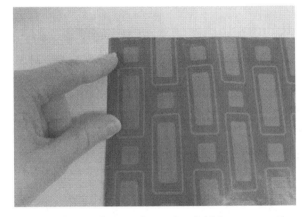

Step 3. Run a finger along the fold to crease the center seam.

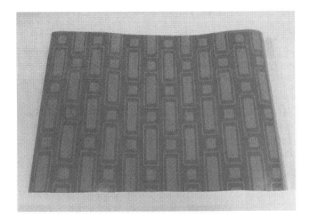

Step 2. Fold the rectangle over, aligning the sides and corners.

Step 4. Open the paper. Lay it flat, pattern side down, on newsprint. Follow the instruction on the can to spray glue on the surface.

Step 5. Carefully pick up the gift wrap and move it to a clean surface.

Step 6. Align the spine of the composition book to the center seam on the gift wrap.

Step 7. Carefully lay down the wrapping paper along one side of the composition book. Try to align the top and bottom seam with the note-book. Work out any bubbles. If lifting the gift wrap up to re-align, do it carefully to keep from making creases in the giftwrap.

Step 8. Repeat for the other side.

Step 10. Protect the work surface. Follow the instruction on the spray adhesive can and spray the back of the plastic pocket.

Step 9. Open the book jacket and work the wrapping paper tightly along the inside cover. Repeat for the other side.

Step 11. Carefully pick up the pocket and place it in the desired location, sticky side down, on the cover of the notebook.

Step 12. Rub the area with fingers to work out any bubbles.

Step 14. If necessary, trim the photograph to fit inside the plastic pocket.

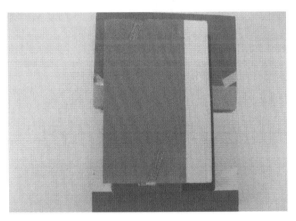

Step 13. Place weeded books as a weight on top of the composition notebook.

Step 15. Slide photograph inside the pocket.

Keyboard Frame

• •

Students are continually trying to take the keys off the keyboards and rearrange them. They seem to be fascinated by the keys. Then one day, students are talking to me about how they would like to spell out words with the keys. So, I began to think, *why not?* I contacted a local recycle center who collects old computer parts, asking if I could have the keys off discarded keyboards. Within a few days they had a large box of keyboards collected for me. I spent a few hours popping keys off the keyboards. Many of them were quite dirty, but easy to clean up by placing the keys in a delicates laundry bag laid on the top shelf of the dishwasher.

Supplies: sandpaper, old picture frame, paper towel, Crayola® Model Magic, recycled computer keyboard keys

Step 1. Take apart an old picture frame. Set aside all but the frame.

Step 2. Sand the frame (even if it is metal).

Step 3. Wipe the frame with a piece of paper towel.

Step 6. With clean and dry hands, roll out a piece of Model Magic the length of the frame. Repeat that for all four sides.

Step 4. Think of a word to place on the frame. Sort through the recycled keys for the letters needed.

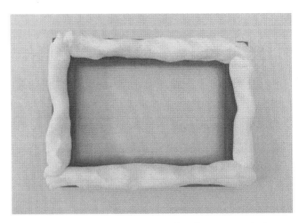

Step 7. Place the rolls onto the frame and shape them into place. Work the Model Magic until the complete surface is covered as evenly as possible.

Step 5. Select four to six non-alphabet keys for corner accents.

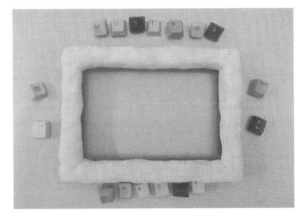

Step 8. Take the selected keys and lay them out along the perimeter of the frame until satisfied with the placement.

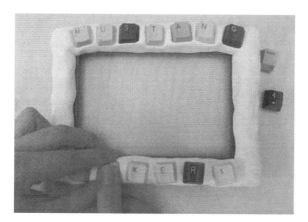

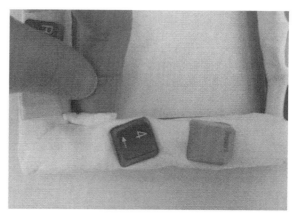

Step 9. Press the keys into the Model Magic, but raised slightly above the Model Magic. To avoid struggling to make a straight line, lay down the keys in a zig-zag, off-kilter manner. Hold the sides of the frame and the dough as you press down to keep the dough from getting mis-formed. Work the Model Magic and keys so that the keys are of even depth.

Step 10. Look at the frame. Roll tiny pieces of Model Magic and work the small pieces into places where the original frame is still showing.

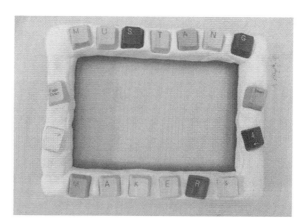

Step 11. Allow for dry time according to the instructions on the Model Magic package.

Library Envelopes

Libraries are continually weeding. Think creatively and consider ways in which part of those books could be reused. Repurpose pages of oversized non-fiction books into envelopes. These envelopes could be made independently or used in conjunction with a card-making make or paper quilt card make. A key to success is making sure the pages of the weeded books are large enough to lay out the envelope template. Also consider the price of postage and use the United States Postal Service® website to look at the most up-to-date rules, ensuring the envelope sizes do not require extra postage.

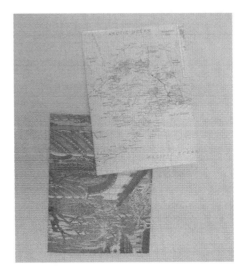

Equipment: scissors, letter opener or other sharp object for taking apart an envelope, pencil

Supplies: store-bought envelope, glue stick, cardstock, weeded non-fiction books with pages large enough to fit the envelope template, recycled paper

United States Postal Service®. "Address Letters & Cards." https://www.usps.com/send/address-letter-cards.htm

Optional Materials: blank address labels

Step 1. Select the appropriate-sized envelope for the letter or card.

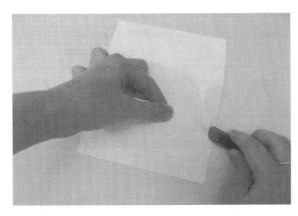

Step 2. Carefully deconstruct the envelope to use as a template.

Step 3. Lay the deconstructed envelope flat on a piece of cardstock. Trace an outline of the envelope onto the cardstock.

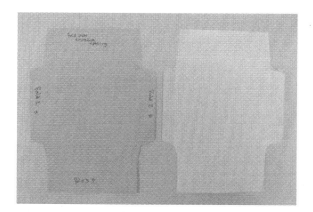

Step 4. Cut out the shape. The cardstock will be the envelope template. Look at the original envelope. Using it as a guide, write on the template the fold instructions.

Step 5. Select a page out of a recycled book to fit the template. Select carefully, considering what image or text will appear on the finished envelope.

Step 6. Lay the envelope on the page to achieve the desired look and trace the outline.

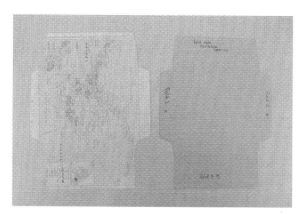

Step 7. Cut out the shape.

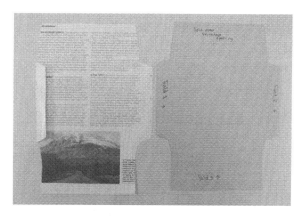

Step 8. Place the cut out on a piece of recycled paper to protect the work surface. Fold the corners of the new envelope to reconstruct the shape of the original envelope. Crease down the edges.

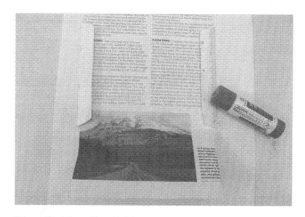

Step 9. Glue the fold seams.

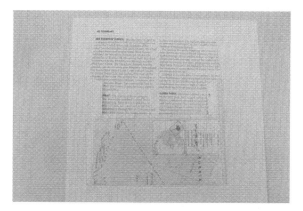

Step 10. Fold up the bottom flap. Press to hold in place until the glue is secure.

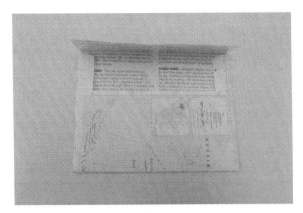

Step 11. Fold down the bottom flap and press down the crease. This is the opening in which to slide the card or letter.

Step 13. Optional: If the design on the front of the envelope is very busy, put an address label in place on which to write the addresses.

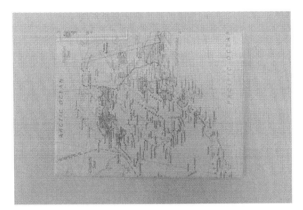

Step 12. Turn the envelope over to address and stamp the front.

Magnetic Poetry

Poetry is an excellent creative venue for the emotional turmoil of the adolescent and teenager. What if they had an outlet for constructing their own poetry? Perry Meridian middle school hosts an annual artists and authors contest and the quality of poetry turned in every year is astounding. But I wanted to take that further and allow for a fun, free-spirited, personal venue for their creativity. That's when I was attending a conference and one of the vendors was giving away a magnetic sheet of tear-away words. *Voila!* Students could make their own magnetic words to put poetry on their locker, refrigerator, or any other magnetic surface they imagine. So now, when magnets are given out at county fairs, businesses, or are free on directories, I explain why I need them and ask if they have any old magnets or extras and I walk away with a large stack of magnets for our project.

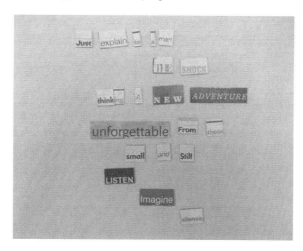

Equipment: scissors, weeded books
Supplies: old magazines and catalogs, used magnet sheets, newsprint, spray adhesive, recycled paper
Optional Materials: industrial paper trimmer, used pocket size tin

Step 1. Go through a catalog or magazine looking for words no taller than ½ inch. Search for a variety of nouns, verbs, descriptive words, conjunctions, etc. Tear out the pages of interest.

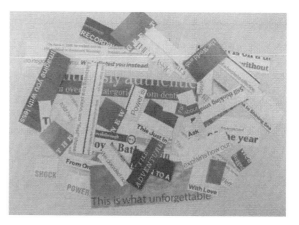

Step 2. Cut out each word along the base of the word, which will help make every word lay on the magnet evenly. Leave a lot of extra space above the word.

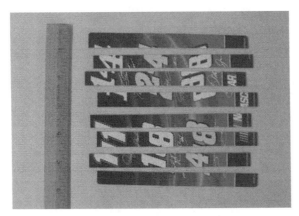

Step 3. Cut the magnet into ½ inch tall strips.

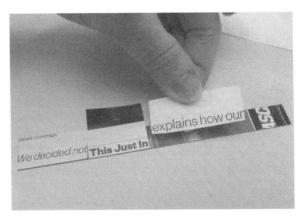

Step 6. Start with one magnet strip. Beginning on one corner, lay one of the word strips with the cutout flush against the bottom edge. Lay the next word strip beside the first one. Repeat until out of space.

Step 4. Lay the strips on newsprint to protect, then follow the instructions on the can to spray adhesive on the surface.

Step 5. Carefully pick up the strips and move them to a piece of recycled paper, sticky side up.

Step 7. Cover with a piece of recycled paper, then stack weeded books on top for weight. Repeat Steps 6 and 7 until all magnetic strips are full.

Step 8. Uncover the strips. With scissors against the magnet edge, trim off the excess paper.

Step 9. Cut the magnet strip into separate words.

Step 11. Optional: Clean a tin container. Store words in the container between use.

Step 10. Cut off the suffix of words to expand the word choices available when building poems.

Money Tin

· ·

As a consumer, consider the packaging of items. Is there some packaging sturdy enough to be repurposed or upcycled? One potential alternative is turning an old metal container into a money box, or other small item catch-all for the pocket, purse, or sports bag. Use containers that, in a previous life, were the package for Altoid mints, small travel puzzles, and other various consumables. Consider the possibilities for redecorating the tin to be personalized and customized.

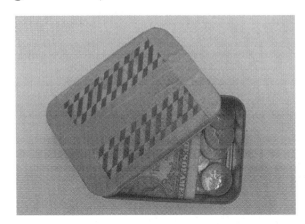

Equipment: scissors, sponge brush
Supplies: pocket-size recycled tin, paper tape, Mod Podge®, recycled paper, paper towel, water, sandpaper

Step 1. Clean the empty tin with a damp paper towel and dry.

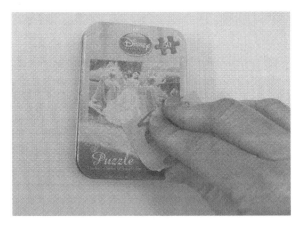

Step 2. Sand the surface of the lid.

Step 3. Select two to four paper tape rolls to decorate the lid.

Step 4. Lay the first piece of tape, cutting the tape so both ends hang off the side of the lid.

Step 5. Complete the pattern, covering the complete surface of the lid.

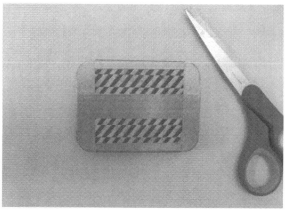

Step 6. Cut the tape along the edge of the lid, carefully cutting off the excess tape.

Step 7. Check the edges to make sure there is no overhanging tape.

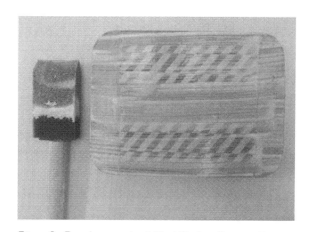

Step 8. Brush a coat of Mod Podge® over the top of the lid and along the side of the lid. Use a finger to wipe off any excess along the lid's ridge. Allow time to dry.

Step 9. Put on a second coat, brushing in the opposite direction. Allow time to dry.

Office Organizer

Students and adults are often looking for interesting and useful ways to keep track of sticky notes and note paper. Something easily carried for jotting down quick messages, reminders and ideas. Incorporate young people's love of craft duct tape and upcycling to create a custom-made office organizer.

Equipment: box cutter, scissors, ruler, pencil

Supplies: newsprint, weeded hardback books, duct tape, five-by-eight-inch notepad with a top seam, various sizes of sticky note pads, unused wallpaper

Optional Materials: pen, masking tape

Step 1. Use the box cutter to cut along the seams of the spine and pull the pages out of the book. Leave only the book cover intact.

Step 2. Cut a piece of duct tape slightly longer than the book and center along the length of the inside of the spine seam. Rub along the tape to help it adhere more firmly.

Step 3. Lay a similar length against the left edge of the tape on the seam.

Step 6. Cut the excess off the bottom edge.

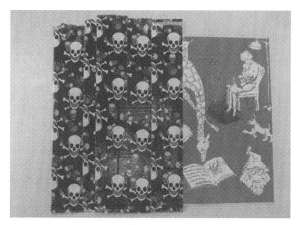

Step 4. Lay a similar length along the left edge of the open book cover. Continue to lay more pieces of tape from the left toward the spine until the left inside is covered.

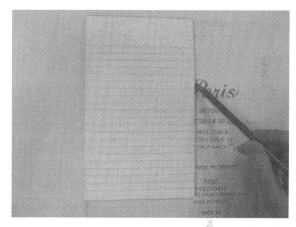

Step 7. Select a piece of wallpaper. Turn it upside down. Trace the outline of the notepad on the wallpaper.

Step 5. Use scissors to cut off the excess along the top edge.

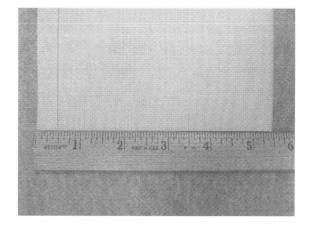

Step 8. Use a ruler to measure out an extra ½ inch for the width. Draw a straight line.

Step 9. Cut out the rectangle along the new lines.

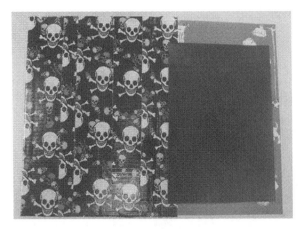

Step 10. Turn the wallpaper over and lay the rectangle on the inside right approximately ½ inch from the bottom and side edge.

Step 11. Cut a new piece of tape to run along the bottom edge of the book, from the right of the spine to past the right side.

Step 13. Lay the strip of tape along the right edge of the book, from the top edge of the wallpaper down to the bottom edge of the book. Be sure the tape is partially laying on the wallpaper to adhere the wallpaper to the inside of the cover.

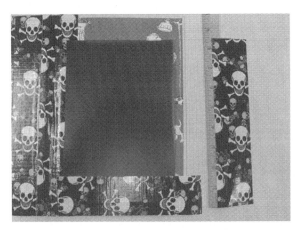

Step 12. Use the ruler to measure from the top edge of the wallpaper to the bottom of the book. Cut a strip of tape that length.

Step 14. Cut another strip of tape the same length and lay it along the left side of the wallpaper and cover in the same fashion.

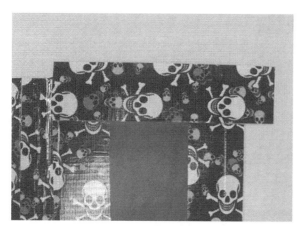

Step 15. Lay a piece of tape along the length of the top of the cover, just above the wallpaper. Be sure not to cover the top opening to the wallpaper.

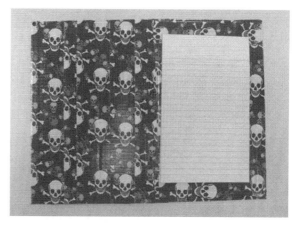

Step 18. Slide the backing of the notepad into the opening at the top of the wallpaper.

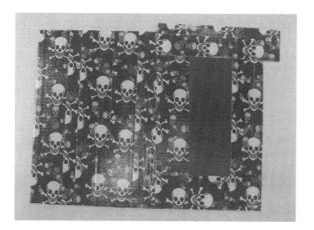

Step 16. Trim off the excess tape along the bottom corner.

Step 17. Trim off the excess tape along the top and top corner and sides.

Step 19. Pull the backs off the sticky note pads and stick to the right of the book. If it does not stick, roll masking tape to the back paper to hold it in place. If book is thin and does not close, remove some of the pages from the sticky note pads until it is able to close properly.

Pencil Case

Most students need a place to store their pens, pencils, and erasers. A container to hold all those little bits and pieces of classroom material is always needed. Participate in an upcycling craft by repurposing a plastic food or drink container with a lid into a pencil case.

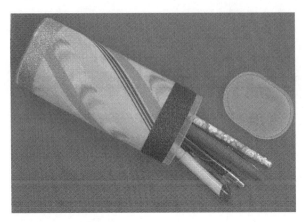

Equipment: scissors, box cutter
Supplies: paper tape, a variety of recycled plastic containers
Optional Materials: craft glue

Step 1. Select a container large enough to hold pens, pencils, and other pencil case supplies. Select a range of aesthetically compatible paper tapes for the length. Select two of the thicker paper tapes for the top and bottom border.

Step 2. Start the tape above the end of one side, wrap it around to the other end. Keep it smooth and free of bubbles.

Step 3. Cut the roll of tape off just past the end of the container.

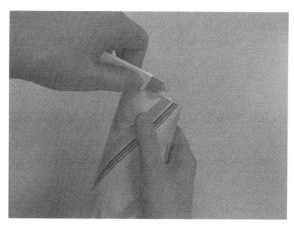

Step 6. Use the box cutter to trim the excess off the bottom edge.

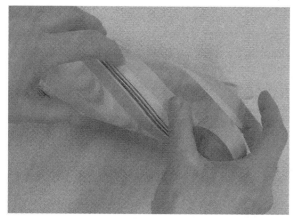

Step 4. Lay the next line of tape next to the edge of the first, continuing to work carefully to ensure the seams touch and no bubbles or wrinkles appear.

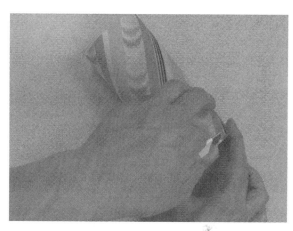

Step 7. Trim the excess off the top edge with the box cutter.

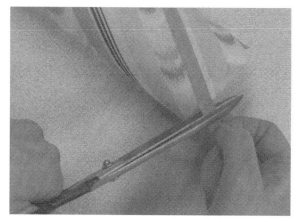

Step 5. Repeat step four until the container is covered. Overlap the last line of tape, if necessary, centering onto the empty space as necessary.

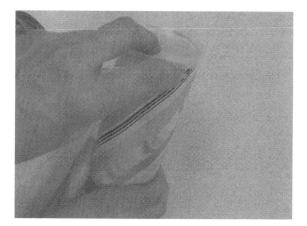

Step 8. Place the lid on the container. Take the box cutter and cut the tape along the edge of the lid, then remove the cut tape.

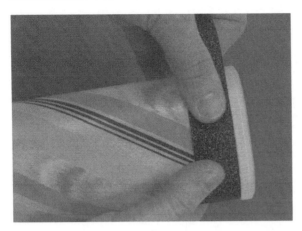

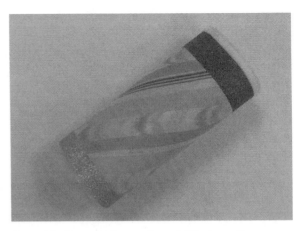

Step 9. With the lid still on, lay the border tape along the length of the base of the lid. Carefully cut with the box cutter to line up the seam.

Step 11. Repeat Steps 9 and 10 along the bottom.

Step 10. Optional: Put a dab of glue along the end of the seam tape and smooth it down.

Tissue Paper Tealight

My student makers wanted to make candle holders, but I wasn't too keen on the idea of an actual candle or matches or fire in school. Adding to my reasoning, even staff having lit candles is against school policy. So what to do? We talked about it and we came up with an agreeable alternative. We used a battery-operated tea light and made a tealight holder. We used old gift bag tissue paper and donated glass food jars with the labels removed. Bulk quantity boxes of battery-operated tea lights can be purchased online or at a local craft store.

Equipment: sponge brush, scissors

Supplies: Mod Podge®, votive glass or small upcycled glass jar, battery-operated tea light, used tissue paper, newsprint

Optional Equipment: circle punch, square punch

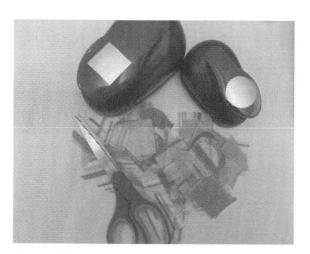

Step 1. Place newsprint on the work surface. Select some tissue paper. Use the scissors or craft punches to cut simple shapes out of the tissue paper.

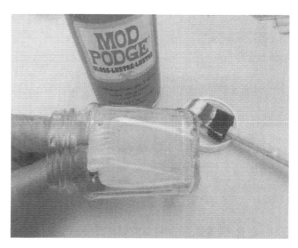

Step 2. Stick fingertips in the jar to hold the jar securely. Coat the outside of the glass with Mod Podge®.

Step 3. Lay pieces of tissue over the Mod Podge® until thoroughly covered. Carefully smooth down pieces without tearing, if possible.

Step 6. Allow time to dry. Repeat the Mod Podge®, brushing in a different direction. Allow time to dry.

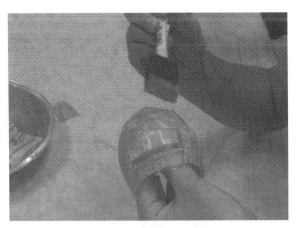

Step 4. Brush a new coat of Mod Podge® over the tissue. Careful to brush in the direction the tissue is laying so as not to cause damage.

Step 7. Turn an electric tea light on and place it in the jar.

Step 5. Place the jar upside down, or in a way that the wet parts will not be touching the newsprint.

Groups

● ●

Group makes are often a large and monumental task. They require a lot of communication, collaboration, and teamwork amongst makers. But for the more complicated makes to work, many first need to learn, in a less stressful make, how to be part of a team and work together effectively. Select some simple make-and-take style activities for dabbling in groups. This is a time for students to work together on a lightweight task. They are not developing technical skills, but instead developing the skills necessary to become a productive member of an effective team. The skills built during these simpler makes can then cross over into the makerspace's more in-depth, lengthy, technical, and challenging group makes.

Recycled Road

This make is inspired by my older brother, Judson Burton, who, in his youth, could spend hours absorbed in creating the most amazing roads, vehicles, and spacecrafts out of upcycled tubes, cups, plates, and Styrofoam packaging.

The fun of playing with toy cars is fairly universal; easy for everyone to understand; and inexpensive, imaginative play. Considering how most people, no matter the age, understand and relate to automobiles, adding them to the fun of the makerspace is a no-brainer. But how difficult would it be to construct a road out of recycled materials where the toy car starts at the top of the road and, with a slight push, is able to make it to the bottom on its own?

For this make, give very few step-by-step guided instructions. Lay out the supplies and beyond the safety rules, list one rule: work as a team to make a road as tall and twisty as possible where the car is able to remain in motion, with no assistance, from the top to the end of the road at the bottom.

Provide miniature toy cars and reuse materials, which could easily be converted into roads, bridges, tunnels, and support pieces. Paper towel tubes could be used to support a road running over the top of it, or holes cut for a road to run through. Paper towel and gift wrapping tubes cut lengthwise could make strips of road. The outer ring of sturdy paper plates could be turned upside down, cut and shaped into twists and turns.

Just for a little fun, take a look at the Jokeroo video and Micro Machine Museum.

- Jokeroo. "Miniature Toy Car Highway." (video) http://www.jokeroo.com/videos/cool/toy-car-highway.html
- Micro Machines Museum. http://m2museum.com

Equipment: micro or mini race cars, scissors, kraft knife or box cutter
Supplies: tape, glue, outer rings cut out of sturdy paper plates (turned upside down to make a road), paper towel tubes, gift wrap paper tubes (cut in half, lengthwise)

Step 1. Using the recycled materials provided, Create a winding road where the car starts at the top and with a slight push, makes it to the bottom.

Step 2. Allow students the freedom to work together to think and create.

Step 3. Host an event day for teams to show off their successful tracks.

Tetrahedron

A tetrahedron is a three-dimensional fractal model. Our tetrahedron was constructed as a school-wide challenge. Every student was asked to cut out a template, write a personal goal on the paper, then seal the goal inside the three-dimensional triangle. They were then left in the workspace in bags and bags of over a thousand colored triangles. Students then came as they could and built the tetrahedron, making it larger and larger every day. For many, it became an obsession in which they couldn't let go, coming before school, during lunch, and after school. The sense of accomplishment was tangible.

Continue to add to the tetrahedron, building as large a structure as possible. This is a make in which a student can come and go, working on the tetrahedron whenever possible, and no matter what phase the project is in, easily jump in as a first-timer or repeat attendee and make sense of the task. This is a visually stunning make in which participants quickly get excited by the growth and visible size as progress is visibly obvious.

- Math is Fun. "Tetrahedron." http://www.mathsisfun.com/geometry/tetrahedron.html
- Museum of Mathematics. "Math Monday: Sierpinski Tetrahedron." http://momath.org/home/math-monday-02-22-10
- Pearsall, Shelley. *All of the Above.* Little Brown Books for Young Readers, 2008.
- Pearsall, Shelley. "Pre-Reading Activities." http://shelleypearsall.com/tetrahedron.pdf
- Yale. "2.C.Similarity Dimension." http://classes.yale.edu/fractals/FracAndDim/SimDim/SimDim.html

Equipment: hot glue gun, tape, copier, scissors
Supplies: glue sticks for glue gun, tetrahedron template, recycled paper, colored paper, cardstock, pencil

Step 1. Make tetrahedron templates out of cardstock and cut out. Use the template to trace tetrahedrons onto recycled paper and colored paper.

Step 2. Use scissors to cut tetrahedrons.

Step 3. Fold the tetrahedron together to make a three dimensional triangle. Use small pieces of tape to tape the sides together.

Step 4. Use the hot glue gun to build a pyramid. Adhere the corners of four triangles together: three as the base, one on top.

Step 5. Take four pyramids made in step four. Glue them together in a similar manner to build a larger pyramid.

Step 6. Take four of the larger pyramids in step five to make an even larger pyramid.

Step 7. Continue in this manner to build the largest tetrahedron possible in the time allotted for the make.

Appendix 1: Glossary

3Doodler—A 3D writing pen that uses ABS (acrylonitrile–butadiene–styreneor) PLA (poly-lactic acid) plastic instead of ink

3D Printer—3D printers range from very large and industrial to desktop. The size of the printer determines the maximum size of the object it can craft. It can be used to create customized parts, design prototypes, models, toys, and much more.

4-H—A national youth organization, with state chapters usually working in partnership with a university. Includes a range of self-directed and mentor-led learning, growth, and make opportunities in a wide range of fields.

Altered Book—Using mixed-media to reimagine a book from its original purpose into something new while retaining some of the original shape.

Altered Craft—Taking an object and changing it to alter its appearance and sometimes changing its function.

Animoto—Web-based video editing platform. Uses uploaded pictures and video, music, and text.

App—Short for application. A program downloaded onto mobile and electronic devices, usually with a very specific, narrow purpose.

Arduino—An open-source programmable microcontroller for prototyping and electronic design.

B-Squares®—Magnetic electronic devices which wirelessly snap together through magnetic contacts into a customizable, technical configuration.

Backstitch—A type of hand stitching commonly used for seams and embroidery.

Baking Extract—a concentrated liquid of a specific flavor, like vanilla.

Beeswax—A wax bees make to construct honeycomb. Beekeepers harvest and process the wax for a variety of uses, including candles, cosmetics, sewing, soaps, and lotions.

Blanket Stitch—A decorative, buttonhole stitch used to hold two pieces together, like the seam of a blanket or pillow.

Cardstock—A thick, heavyweight paper used in scrapbooking, card making, and other crafts.

Circuit Board—An insulated board on which circuits and components are mounted. Today this often includes microchips.

Cloud Computing—Accessing or storing programs and files over a network, often through the Internet.

Coil-less or Coiless Safety Pin—A safety pin used in a variety of crafts. More versatile for various projects than the standard safety pin because there is no loop, or coil, at the end opposite of the clasp.

Conductive Fabric—Fabric which is capable of carrying an electrical current for e-textiles.

Contact Paper—Sold in the housewares or kitchen department and traditionally used to line the surface of shelves and drawers. Contact paper has a peel-away back to expose an adhesive and the front is often a vinyl-like texture sold in a variety of colors and patterns.

Cowl Scarf—A scarf with the ends connected to make a tube.

167

Creative Commons—A Creative Commons (CC) license allows the creator to control how music, video, code, text, and art may be attributed, shared, and distributed.

Cutting Mat—A protective surface on which to cut fabric, paper, and other objects. Often the mat is self-healing and frequently used with a rotary cutter.

Decoupage Glue—A craft glue used to adhere items to an object. It is often also used as a sealant. Decoupage glue can be made by thinning regular school glue. The most widely recognized decoupage glue is Mod Podge®.

Digital Badge—An electronic representation of a patch or certificate earned. Badges are earned and represent the accomplishment of a task, training, or the expertise in a subject.

DIY Couture—"Do it yourself" fashion by designing and constructing clothing, jewelry, hats, shoes, and accessories.

Dominoes—A tile game played by two or more people. Dominoes sets range from the double sixes, double nines, double twelve, double fifteen, and double eighteen. The smaller the set, the fewer people playing.

Duct Tape—An adhesive tape frequently used for temporary home repairs, but now comes in a variety of colors and patterns for crafting. Duck® Tape is the most recognized brand of duct tape.

Couture—Custom-made clothing fitted specifically for the individual.

eBook—A book in electronic form.

E-textiles—Combining sewing with electronics: wearable electronics sewn, knitted, or woven into clothing, hats, shoes, or accessories.

Embroidery—Decorative needlework traditionally hand-stitched, but now also done with computerized sewing machines.

Embroidery Hoop—Two snug fitting hoops. A fabric is placed between the two hoops to hold it taut and in place for handiwork like stitching and beading.

Essential Oil—An aromatic oil obtained from plants and used for a variety of purposes, including adding scents to body products like soaps, moisturizers, and lip balms.

Fab Lab—A fabrication laboratory whose purpose is to support and encourage modern invention and personal fabrication through sharing tools and facilities.

Fabric Stabilizer—Used for embroidery and sewing to make the fabric more rigid while sewing. Once the work is complete, it is torn away or washed away to reveal the final product.

Fabrication—Manufacturing, making or creating something.

Freeform Sewing—Sewing without making or using a traditional pattern.

French Jewelry Pin—See coil-less safety pin.

Glue Dots®—Convenient circles of double-sided, clear adhesive for arts and crafts. Available in repositionable, permanent, acid free and a range of sizes.

Graphic Novel—A full-length book told in pictures and words. Much like a comic book, both the images and text are integral to the reader fully comprehending the story.

Green—Incorporating organic, natural, and recycled into the make.

Instructable—Originally a website for sharing projects. The word is now becoming synonymous with a type of how-to guide where the step-by-step instructions include images and text for each step of the process.

Ironing Mat—A pad which can be laid down on any surface to protect it while using a hot iron.

K'NEX™—A construction toy of rods, tubes, and connectors for building movable machines and stationary buildings and objects.

Knitting Loom—A round or oblong plastic or wood frame with short rods protruding from the top. It is an alternate form of knitting from the traditional knitting needles.

Kodu Game Lab—Allows users to make games for the PC or Xbox with little or no previous programming experience.

LilyPad—A microcontroller which combines art and technology with a board designed for wearables and e-textiles.

littleBits—Snap-together electronic modules programmable through an open source library.

Loom Hook—A hand tool with a bent metal stem on the end for hooking and moving yarn on a knitting loom.

Loom Knitting—It is an alternate form of knitting from the traditional knitting needles, instead using a knitting loom and loom hook to knit.

Loop Knot—A loop knot is used to begin knitting and is considered the first stitch.

Mah-Jongg—A Chinese tile game traditionally played with dice, 144 tiles, and four people.

Make and Take—Simplified activities that can usually be made in one visit.

MakerBot®—A desktop 3D printer.

Merit Badge—Recognition for completing, learning, or doing something requiring learning, developing skills, and deserving of recognition.

Micro-Manufacturing—Manufacturing on a small scale.

Microwave Flower Press—A microwave-safe container for pressing flowers in an expedited, more immediate, manner using a microwave.

Mindstorm—Lego® Software and hardware used to create programmable robots.

Miter Box—A metal box with built-in straight and angled guides for cutting small objects with a hand saw.

Mod Podge®—Often used in decoupage and other crafts. Since the 1960s, Mod Podge® has been marketed as a water base, non-toxic, all-purpose crafting glue, sealer, and finisher all in one. A wide range of Mod Podge® is available for different surfaces, including fabric, glass, and paper. It also comes in different lusters, including glossy, matte, sparkle, satin, shimmer, as well as hard coat, outdoor, and puzzle saver.

Newsprint—An inexpensive, oversized, low quality paper made from wood and recycled materials.

Open Source Hardware—Electronic or computer hardware available free.

Paper Quilt—Quilting done with paper and a sewing machine instead of fabric. Most often used to create greeting cards, gift cards, and fine art for framing.

Paper Tape—A crafting tape with a color and design on one side and adhesive on the other. Often purchased in rolls much the size and shape of traditional masking tape. Used in scrapbooking, card making, and other paper crafts as well as for children's games and hobbies.

Paper Trimmer—A portable, desktop, straight-edge cutting tool.

Parchment Paper—Baking parchment paper is used in baking and crafts. It is sometimes thought of as wax-less wax paper and is resistant to moisture and grease.

Pattern—A guide for making something.

Plarn—Yarn for knitting, crochet, weaving, and other crafts made by upcycling plastic bags. Thickness of the plarn is dependent upon the width of the strips cut.

Polyurethane—A top-coat resin varnish for protecting surfaces of projects from heat, water, and other elements.

Pony Bead—Barrel-shaped plastic or glass beads. Pony beads are used for a variety of crafts as well as in jewelry and are available in a range of colors and transparencies.

ProtoSnap—Intended for wearable e-textiles and to teach Arduino programming simply, which does not require soldering or wiring. Everything is already wired on a single board.

Prototype—An original used as a model for manufacturing. 3D printers can be used in a maker-space for creating prototypes.

Robot—A machine programmed to perform a task.

Rotary Cutter—A circular blade attached to a handle. Used in conjunction with a cutting mat to cut items like paper and fabric.

Sealant—A spray or paint used to seal or protect the surface of a completed project.

Seam—The place where two pieces, like cloth or felt, are joined together.

Slipknot—A knot with a loop which, when no longer needed, is easily untied.

Soft Circuit—Electronics sewn into clothing using conductive threads.

Solder—Fusing together two metal objects.

STEM—In education, STEM is an acronym for teaching, learning, and motivating interest in the fields of science, technology, engineering, and math.

Straight Stitch—Also called a flat stitch. It is a stitch made by hand or with a machine, keeping the thread in a straight line, hence the name straight stitch. It is often used in hems and to sew two pieces together.

Storyboard—A form of graphic organizer used to depict the action sequences for a video or video slide show.

Textile—A fabric

Trivet—An object used to protect table and counter surfaces from hot objects, like pans, during the cooking and servicing process.

Upcycling—Taking recycled objects and reusing all or parts for other purposes.

Video Slideshow—A video make with a sequence of still images, text and sound (narration and/or music).

Vinyl Paper—A peel and stick water-resistant, tear-resistant paper.

Washi Tape—A brand of craft paper tape (see Paper Tape).

Weaving Loom—A device for holding thread, yarn, or fabric for weaving.

Witch Hazel—A liquid made from the witch-hazel shrub. Often used as an astringent, soother, or in body care products.

Wite-Out®—A name brand for correction fluid originally intended for office work to remove imperfections from a page or business document.

XBee—An XBee module works in conjunction with an Arduino board. The module receives then sends data to the board.

Zigzag Stitch—It is a stitch usually made by a machine, moving the thread forward in a zig-zag pattern, hence the name zigzag stitch.

Appendix 2: National and Local Events & Contests

Consider getting involved in or attending local and national events. It is a way to learn, be inspired, grow a basic skill base as program coordinator, as well as share and publicize the activities and successes of library makerspace participants.

Some events offer materials with registration. If not just attending as an observer, but participating, review the participation policies to ensure the school library makerspace can meet the obligations placed when registering and accepting the organization's free or reduced-fee materials, supplies, and promotional support.

4-H County Fair—http://www.4-h.org/   The 4-H fair in your region is a valuable resource for science, craft, community, and hobby projects and activities created by young people, as well as adult mentors and subject-related organizations. Projects created in the makerspace could be shared through 4-H fair project entry. A directory of training materials on a variety of subjects can also be found at http://www.4-hdirectory.org. Subject categories include agriculture science, animal science, citizenship, communication and expressive arts, consumer and family science, earth and space science, environmental science, food and nutrition, health and fitness, leadership, personal development, plant science, technology and engineering, volunteer development, and workforce preparation.

4-H National Youth Science Day—http://www.4-h.org/4-h-national-youth-science-day/nysd home.aspx   Intended to spark an interest in science, science careers in youth, and science exploration. With goals focusing on STEM (science, technology, engineering, and math), each year an annual theme and date is announced. Free resources include videos, images, experiment guides, planning and promotional materials, and an archive of materials from all past years. Project kits are available for a fee. If unable to participate on the official 4-H National Youth Science Day, event planners are encouraged to use any other dates for the event which best fit individual program schedules. To access all materials on the site, register and complete a profile. Read the 4-H Council terms and conditions during registration to confirm understanding and compliance to the regulations.

Arbor Day—http://www.arborday.org/arborday/   Annually, the last Friday in April is the official national Arbor Day, but check the website to see which states have an adjusted date due to optimal tree-planting times. The website includes the history and origin of Arbor Day, classroom connections by content area, suggestions for how to participate locally, and a downloadable guidebook.

Craftster Challenge—http://www.craftster.org/forum/index.php?board=174.0#axzz2OTH4s AnG   The Craftster community hosts a monthly craft challenge. To enter the challenge, create a project based on the posted theme, rules, and entry procedures. Encouraging ethical behavior, it is important to note that citing sources for concept inspiration is encouraged. After the deadline, projects are voted on, and prizes awarded.

Digital Learning Day—http://www.digitallearningday.org/   Digital Learning Day is a national event for K-12 schools to celebrate the use of technology in education. Included is information for various participant coordinators, news, events, lessons, and showcases. Sign up through the website for updates, news, and events.

Digital Media + Learning Competition (DML)—http://www.dmlcompetition.net   An annual competition with a financial award. Organizations, including libraries, complete proposals for youth programmers to participate in hands-on learning experiences. The website includes application, judging criteria, participation design guidelines, and more.

Free Comic Book Day—http://www.freecomicbookday.com   The first Saturday in May is a day when local comic book stores give away free comics. Work with a local comic book store to collaborate between the store's Free Comic Book Day event and makerspace programming. Use the resources provided on the website to enrich the makerspace activities.

Google Science Fair—https://www.google.com/intl/en/events/sciencefair/index.html   Through a partnership with Cern, Lego®, National Geographic, and Scientific American™, Google takes the science fair concept digital with an international science competitions for teens through age eighteen. The website provides information about rules and regulations, guidelines, registration, judging, and educator tools. Although projects do not have to be technological, the contest is virtual: enter through the Google Science Fair platform and submission guidelines.

I Love Yarn Day—www.craftyarncouncil.com/i-love-yarn   The Craft Yarn Council sponsors a day celebrating yarn every fall. On this day, people are asked to share their love of yarn by wearing, sharing, and making crafts with yarn. This is an opportunity to open the makerspace to a variety of yarn-related options which then can be traded throughout the school or donated to a local organization on I Love Yarn Day.

Instructables—http://www.instructables.com/contest/   Instructibles hosts a wide range of themed contests with various deadlines throughout the year, as well as links to hundreds of other national contests. An invaluable resource for sharing maker projects in every imaginable and unimaginable subject.

International Gaming Day—http://ngd.ala.org/   International Gaming Day is sponsored by the American Library Association. Although officially held on the third Saturday in November, registered libraries are encouraged to register and host the event as close to the official date as possible. Included are a press kit, tournament details, and registration information. Sign up to receive email updates, which will remind you when registration has opened and much more. Consider this an opportunity for students to improve, share, and grow skills by creating, contributing, and leading games of their own making.

International Space Apps Challenge—http://spaceappschallenge.org/   A forty-eight-hour worldwide event. Challenges, projects, and a list of participating locations are included.

Make to Learn Youth Contest—http://www.instructables.com/contest/maketolearn/ Young makers share a project made, answer four questions related to the project, and create a how-to for others to follow. Open to young people under the age of eighteen. This meets all four Learning 4Life goals: think, create, share, and grow.

Maker Faire—http://makerfaire.com/ Maker Faires and mini–Maker Faires are sponsored by Maker Media, and are the brain child of *Make* magazine and O'Reilly Media. A Maker Faire bring makers and maker-enthusiasts together in a convention, county fair, exhibition, festival-like, family-friendly atmosphere. The website provides information about upcoming faires throughout the world as well as how to host a community faire in your own region.

NASA Centennial Challenge—http://www.nasa.gov/directorates/spacetech/centennial_chal lenges/index.html/ Since 2005, NASA has sponsored a series of competitions to encourage innovative solutions to scientific problems. Prizes are offered for each challenge. Each challenge includes registration, competition summary, rules, and youth ambassadors.

National Sewing Month—http://www.nationalsewingmonth.org/index.html Since 2008, National Sewing Month includes a contest, free theme-related projects, articles, and much more. Traditionally held in September, each year a new theme is adopted. It is sponsored by the American Sewing Guild and the Sewing and Craft Alliance.

National STEM Video Game Challenge—http://stemchallenge.org/ Middle and high school students are challenged to create a video game of original design. The website includes mentors, expert tips, and the students section describes important details, including game-design platforms, game design, and game making tools.

PTO Today—www.ptotoday.com From the website find the link to the Free School Program page. PTO Today is hosted by School Family Media, Inc., with the intent to provide resources and opportunities for supporting school parent groups. As of this publication, opportunities include family events on food and nutrition, science, and Kinect™ Family Game Night. When registering directly on the website for each individual program, be prepared to report which month and year the program will occur. An email confirmation will be sent with a link to downloadable online resources which include planning materials, games and activities, and other project-specific documents. A kit of other program-specific materials will be shipped directly to the registered address closer to the provided event date. A person is required to be a member of the local PTA/PTO group in order to register.

Stamping, Stationery, and Scrapbooking **Magazine**—http://www.hobbylobby.com/project _inspiration/customer_projects/customer_project_form.cfm A paper crafting project, of original design only, can be entered for submission into Hobby Lobby®'s national papercrafting magazine. The magazine comes out quarterly and the website clearly lists quarterly submission deadlines, rules, and links to entry forms.

Teen Tech Week—http://teentechweek.ning.com/ An annual week of library programming dedicated to teen use of technology in libraries. Every library is encouraged to celebrate in their own way and the website offers resources, ideas, a forum, and much more. This event is sponsored by YALSA (Young Adult Library Services Association). Along with other Teen Tech Week activities, this is a week to showcase all the completed technology-related makerspace projects from throughout the year.

World Environment Day—http://www.unep.org/wed/about/   Sponsored by the United Nations, World Environment Day (WED) is held worldwide June 5. It is a day when environmental awareness activities are to culminate in a community call to action day.

Appendix 3:
Ideas and Inspirations

Sometimes all it takes is a spark to be inspired. Utilize these resources to locate activities and supplies for your makerspace. This is not a comprehensive list, but a starting point to motivate programming ideas. Often what is seen is not what works for every makerspace, but instead an inspiration for a blending, or smash-up, of a variety of makerspace ideas. Create a melting pot of notions with what supplies are available, or can easily be collected, and you can afford to add to the makerspace for an activity.

If choosing an activity out of the realm of personal experience, try starting from a kit. A kit includes all materials and often includes clear, guided instructions. Read descriptions carefully as some kits come with necessary tools, yet with others, tools will be an additional, necessary purchase.

3Doodler—http://www.the3doodler.com/   The 3Doodler is a 3D writing pen that uses ABS or PLA plastic instead of ink and does not require a computer, programming, software, or any technical knowledge. An interesting way to sample 3D art and design without the larger expense of a 3D printer. To stay informed, subscribe to the email newsletter.

AASL Best Apps for Teaching and Learning—http://www.ala.org/aasl/guidelines/best-apps A list updated annually of twenty-five apps to foster inquiry, innovative teaching, active student engagement, and curriculum development which support AASL's *Standards for the 21st Century Learner*.

AASL Best Websites for Teaching and Learning—http://www.ala.org/aasl/guidelinesand standards/bestlist/bestwebsites   A list updated annually of the top twenty-five websites recognized for their innovative approach to inquiry based learning, active engagement, and participation of user. They are free, web-based, and personify the AASL's *Standards for the 21st Century Learner*.

Aerbook Maker—http://aerbook.com/site/   Use Aerbook Maker to build ebooks and apps without the need to write code. An ebook can include text, video, and audio, with the option to add depth, motion, interactivity, and elements. All projects are made in the browser and saved in the cloud. Apps are exported in Corona format. Play around with a free account before using the contact information on the website for school pricing.

All Free Craft—http://www.allfreecrafts.com/kids/index.shtml   This website promises to deliver free craft projects and patterns. Projects are sorted by patterns, holiday, craft projects, and green projects, then divided further within those categories. Most projects include a written description, images of the final product, supply list, and instructions. Although the projects are considered appropriate for younger children, many lend themselves to skill building, training, and interests of teenagers as well.

Arduino—http://www.arduino.cc/   Arduino are open-source microcontroller boards for prototyping and electronic design. They are intended to simplify electronics for artists, hobbyists, tinkerers, and makers. The website includes a learning page. Also see the Appendix 3 entry for SparkFun for more user-friendly guidance; helpful for those with little or no experience using or teaching the hardware or software.

B-Squares™—http://www.b-squares.com/   Magnetic electronic devices which wirelessly snap together through magnetic contacts into customizable, technical configuration without the need for soldering. Snap the squares together to build the outcome needed. The modular devices available are Arduino, battery, bluetooth, dock, LED, proto, solar, and speaker.

Better Homes & Gardens® Do-It-Yourself Decorating—http://www.bhg.com/decorating/do-it-yourself/   Videos, instructions, demonstrations, and visuals for many do-it-yourself home, repurposing, updating, and art projects. Included are tutorials to build particular skills and helpful guidance for learning how to safely use particular tools. Sign up for the DIY Newsletter to receive weekly updates for DIY, crafts, or home improvement.

Can*Teen Challenges—http://www.canteengirl.org/challenges/   Can*Teen is Carnegie Science Center's Chevron Center for STEM Education and Career Development project. The goal is to encourage female teen and tween interest in STEM-related careers. The Challenges are STEM-related activities covering a variety of topics and hands-on experiences.

Craft Elf—http://www.craftelf.com/   Craft Elf is a wealth of craft and hobby ideas and instructions. Each project includes a supply list and step-by-step instructions and images. All projects are sorted into general crafts, sewing, party, holiday, crochet, seasonal, and knitting. General training include sewing and crochet abbreviations and terms, and knitting abbreviations and terms. The handy list of craft hints and tips range from cutting Styrofoam, using a hot glue gun, using a paint squeeze bottle correctly, dry brush techniques, and much more.

Cut Out + Keep: Make and Share Craft Tutorials—http://www.cutoutandkeep.net/   Established in 2007, this website is based out of England. It hosts the online magazine, *Snippets*, and over sixty-one thousand step-by-step craft tutorials. This is a site to learn how to make something, be inspired by another craft, or contribute a step-by-step tutorial. Categories include art, beauty, cooking, crochet, decorating, DIY for the home, dressmaking, fashion, jewelry, knitting, needlework, papercraft, sewing, and yarncraft.

DIY Couture—http://www.diy-couture.co.uk/home.html   A new way for sewing clothing. Instead of the traditional tissue paper sewing pattern to place, pin, and cut, purchasing a pattern gives instructions through diagrams and pictures. This is a forward-thinking way to re-invent the craft of sewing into a new, more accessible manner. Sample patterns and simple sewing lessons are free on the website. Also available is a companion book, *DIY Couture: Create Your Own Fashion Collection* by Rosie Martin (2012).

Evil Mad Scientist Laboratories—http://www.evilmadscientist.com/   Follow the link to the blog hosted by a family-owned, California-based business to encourage and create tinkering scientists everywhere. They also accept and post others' creations. Products available for purchase through the website are various kits, components, and accessories.

FabLab Projects—http://academy.cba.mit.edu/classes/index.html   The Fab Lab Academy class list links to information about fabrication tools and concepts.

Hobby Lobby® Project: Inspiration™—http://www.hobbylobby.com/project_inspiration /project_inspiration.cfm   The Hobby Lobby™ craft store hosts a project inspiration website. Projects can be found by browsing by season, category, or viewing a list. The projects come in a PDF ready-to-print format. The project sheets are heavy on visuals and highly inspirational with a variety of ideas utilizing the same techniques. Some project sheets lack step-by-step instructions and assume a level of comfort and understanding with the topic.

Howtoons—http://www.howtoons.com/   Howtoons is an incredibly creative and fun website. A collaborative group, including a toy designer, comic book artist, inventor, and others come together to share graphically through comics, how to create. It is a stimulating combination of visual and text instruction in an entertaining, comic book format. Project ideas can be searched by material, topic, or title. A glossary is included.

The Home Depot® Workshops—http://workshops.homedepot.com/workshops   Need to bone up on some of skills before rolling out a project concept to students? The Home Depot® frequently hosts DIY live, in-store workshops for adults. The website also provides a wealth of online video project, skills guides, and blog at the Project How-To site. http://www6.home depot.com/how-to/index.html.

Instructables—http://www.instructables.com/   A place to find or contribute projects and how-to makes with photos, step-by-step instruction, or video. Projects are divided into categories: ebooks, technology, workshop, living, food, play, and outside. There are forums for sharing and resources for teachers. Currently, Instructables offers educators free pro membership.

Jo-Ann Fabric and Craft Stores®—http://www.joann.com/project-home/   Not just an online craft and hobby store, their online projects website is organized into twenty-seven categories and sortable by time required to complete the activity and skill level. Each project includes an image of the completed item, supplies and tools list, and step-by-step instructions. Videos are also available on YouTube through *Learn with Jo-Ann*: http://www.youtube.com/user/Joanndotcom.

Kaboose—www.kaboose.com   A website from Disney with food, crafts, and games. Activities are often overly simple, but inspirational for developing more complicated and skills building activities. Also hosts Kaboose TV, which includes craft how-to videos.

K'NEX®—http://www.knex.com   K'NEX® building products include the traditional, construction sets of K'NEX®, Lincoln Logs®, and Tinker Toy®. The website includes products and purchasing, including kits. The educators section contains grant writing help, lesson plans, standards alignment (including STEM), a product matrix, information about regional training conferences, and more. Free registration promises access to sample lesson plans, ideas and information on K'NEX® Building Challenges, and special offers only available through email.

Kodu Game Lab—http://fuse.microsoft.com/projects/kodu   Kodu is a free PC download which allows users to make games for the PC or Xbox with little or no previous programming experience. Included in the website are training videos, instruction and help sheets in PDF, and a classroom kit with lesson plans and activities. Go to the Kodu Game Lab Community to see examples: http://www.kodugamelab.com/.

Lego® Digital Designer—http://ldd.lego.com   A free download from the website, Lego® Digital Designer allows for custom design of Lego® models, including Mindstorms. Along with the custom creation of a model, building instructions are produced, and completed models and instructions can be uploaded and shared at the website.

Lego® Education—http://www.legoeducation.us/   Associated with robotics competitions for elementary, middle, and high school students, this website supports preschool through university-level learning through hands-on construction of robotic technologies, machine sets, Legos, and classroom activities and curriculum. Subscribe to the Lego® Education News to stay informed of deals, new products, competitions, and curriculum resources.

LibraryThing Edible Book Contest—http://www.librarything.com/   Begun in 2012, Library-Thing hosts an annual edible book contest every spring. To enter, create a book-inspired edible, then send a picture and caption by the due date.

Lion Brand® Yarns—http://www.lionbrand.com/   From the website, there are free crochet, knitting, and craft patterns. Others are available for purchase for crochet, knitting, and loom knitting. Also included is a blog and helpful learning center, including a video library. To access patterns, even free patterns, requires free registration and optional subscriptions to various email newsletters. Available for purchase are kits, supplies, tools, and online classes.

littleBits—http://shop.littlebits.com/   littleBits are electronic modules and the website has an opensource library of projects, lessons, products, and kits. A value of littleBits is that no programming skills or soldering is required. The circuit-board pieces literally snap together to make a larger circuit. These pieces can light, sound, motor, pulse, and much more. An ingenious way to modernize the circuit board to make creating and constructing a safer environment for schools.

Lowe's® Build and Grow®—http://lowesbuildandgrow.com   Free project clinics for kids. The classes usually focus on woodworking projects, are for kids' grade 1-5, and include a completion patch, the project kit, and use of all necessary tools. Although the clinics are for younger kids, the beginning woodworking workshop kits are design inspiration and can be purchased from http://www.lowes.com/Tools/Kids-Tools-Building-Kits/Kids-Woodworking-Project-Kits.

Lowe's® Creative Ideas for Home and Garden®—http://www.lowescreativeideas.com   A do-it-yourself center for home improvement and craft projects divided into the categories of indoor space, outdoor space, and weekend projects. Included is an inspiration center. Click on

Indoor Spaces or Outdoor Spaces to see a visual listing of some DIY projects. Each project includes photos of the final project, skill level, estimated cost and time, and a list of supplies and other project resources. Step-by-step instructions are included as necessary and some include how-to videos. Under Weekend Projects click on Beginner for woodworking skills videos. Register online for free subscriptions to *Lowe's Creative Ideas for Home and Garden* and *Lowe's Creative Ideas for Your New Home* magazines at http://lowescreativeideas.com/extras.aspx.

Make and Takes™—http://www.makeandtakes.com/   A parenting website full of simple crafts, projects, recipes, and holiday ideas. Includes ideas to use as-is or easily adapted for school makerspaces. Subscribe to the electronic newsletter for regular updates.

Make Projects—http://makeprojects.com/   Project ideas shared by the maker community on a website hosted by *Make* magazine. The list of projects continues to expand as makers share an assortment of ideas. Your makers could contribute to the community with a successful project from the school library makerspace.

Maker Shed—http://www.makershed.com/   Maker Shed is an online store for pre-packaged maker activities. This is an ideal place for getting jump-start ideas and materials to help fledgling makerspaces and for guidance to young makers who are just getting started. Available for purchase are crafts, kits, tools, electronics, books, magazines, and much more.

MakerBot®—http://www.makerbot.com/   With the development of the Replicator™ desktop 3D printer and MakerBot® Customizer app, which simplifies 3D design, 3D printing is possible in smaller communities and makerspaces. Included in the website is a store for printers and filament (printing supplies), a community, newsletter, video for further learning, understanding, and exploring of the 3D printing experience.

Makerspace: Sample Projects—http://makerspace.com/projects/sample-projects and http://makerspace.com/category/projects   Makerspace shares a range of digital, manufacturing, and science maker crafts. Included are instructions, videos, pictures, and project kits available for purchase through the Maker Shed.

The McCall Pattern Company: Shops at McCall—http://shops.mccall.com/   McCall's® is a trusted name in design and manufacturer of sewing patterns, but this is no longer your grandmother's sewing company. The *Shops@Mcall* website is sorted into two major categories: sewing and paper crafts. Each of those sections is broken down further into smaller categories. Although this is a website devoted to shopping and incredibly comprehensive, it is also useful for browsing and being inspired to try a new makerspace craft or for learning about or finding just the right equipment or tool. There are so many advancements in technology and tools which are innovating and re-invigorating traditional crafts; this website is ideal for browsing and learning that a piece of equipment or tool exists to move that craftsmanship of a hobby into the twenty-first century.

Menards®—http://www.menards.com/main/howtoguides.html   Menards home improvement store website offers up a wide range of free how-to videos. Included are garden and outdoor, home and décor, and building materials.

Michaels®—http://www.michaels.com/Projects/projects,default,sc.html   Michaels stores companion projects website. Divided into sixteen categories, mainly by craft type but also including a teacher and webisodes category. Category searches can be further narrowed by time required to complete and recommended age level for the craft. Each craft includes a description summary, time estimate, an image of completed project, supply list, and step-by-step instructions.

Michaels® Show IN Tell—http://www.michaels.com/Store-Events/store-events,default,pg .html   Michaels® stores throughout the country host in-store workshops and demonstrations. Usually held on Saturdays or Sundays, most events are free, although some, like the Scrap-IN, have a nominal fee and require advance registration. Check the website for upcoming topics, dates, and times, and check with local stores to confirm attendance policy and procedures. This would be a way to review skills, learn new techniques, or experience new crafts before implementing them into the school library makerspace.

MIT AppInventor—http://appinventor.mit.edu/teach/   With a Google account, students create mobile apps. Lessons for getting started, resources, and guides for classrooms and workshop leaders. A description and helpful video for understanding, as well as valuable tutorials, are available at http://appinventor.mit.edu/explore/.

Our Best Bites—http://www.ourbestbites.com/category/crafts-and-family-fun/   Two working moms come together to create a website devoted to food and fun. Includes a recipe index, links to giveaways, crafts, tips, and tutorials. Be sure to take a good, long look at the Crafts and Family Fun printables.

Paper by Fifty Three—http://www.fiftythree.com/paper   A 2012 App of the Year for iPad, this lets you use a finger or stylus to sketch, draw, write, color, or outline. Draw is free, but essentials, mixer, color, sketch, write, and outline are add-ons for purchase. This takes the doing from traditional to technological, yet still has the same powerful impact of creating, thinking, and expressing.

Plug and Wear—http://www.plugandwear.com/   Technology has broken into the textile world and this company based out of Italy has been dedicated to wearable technology for over fifty years. Kits, components, fabrics, wires, thread, and microcontrollers are available for purchase. Included are a range of basic tutorials on the following subjects: light emitting fabrics, pressure sensitive fabrics and tape, conductive fabrics, and kits. The website includes a handy currency converter for the ease of US purchasing.

Pottery Barn Kids—http://www.potterybarnkids.com/customer-service/store-events.html   Although Pottery Barn Kids events and activities are intended for much younger children, checking out events at nearby stores could provide the makerspace program coordinator inspiration for ideas which can be upscaled to fit older children.

Purdue University: Indiana 4-H Youth Development—http://www.four-h.purdue.edu /projects/index.cfm   The local 4-H organization is a gateway to persons in many fields of expertise and ideas for makerspace collaborations. A range of 4-H projects align with the makerspace philosophy and project manuals can be helpful for makers and mentors. Coordinate makerspace activities with regional 4-H offices to collaborate activities with potential projects for local 4-H fair judging. The partnership would be a valuable community connection between the school library and 4-H by building a fan base of new or existing 4-H participants. To find a local 4-H connection, search the national 4-H website: http://www.4-h.org/.

Sewing and Craft Alliance—http://www.sewing.org/   The website includes sewing education, free sewing and craft projects, articles, a blog, holiday projects, kids and teen projects, charitable projects, and much more. Included is a link for finding a sewing teacher. An email newsletter is also available.

Soft Circuit Saturdays—http://softcircuitsaturdays.com/   An award-winning website hosted by an e-textile maker. This is a website which explores craft technology and wearable computing. Included are reactive fashion designs, tutorials, weekend builds, events, research and reviews, hardware, and DIY resources.

SparkFun® Electronics—http://www.sparkfun.com/   An online shopping center for electronics for the modern and inexperienced through the advanced maker. Online tutorials are available for free. Attend web classes for a fee. A wide range of electronics tutorial topics available for beginner through advanced, include Arduino, prototyping, XBees®, LilyPad, soldering, ProtoSnap, Soft Circuits, and much more. Currently, educator discounts are available for products and classes.

Spoonful—http://spoonful.com/   A website and newsletter sponsored by Disney. Included are cooking, craft, and game ideas, some of which are easily adaptable to the maker.

Thingiverse—http://www.thingiverse.com/   Thingiverse is the companion website to browse and explore the MakerBot® 3D printing world. Available from here is the MakerBot® Customizer™ app as well as other apps and other digital designs shared from all over the world.

Upcycle Magazine—http://www.upcyclemagazine.com/   Included in this handy website are upcycling do-it-yourself projects submitted by readers or found and recommended from throughout the Internet. Categories range from crafts, sewing, gardening, jewelry, clothing, furniture, cooking, art, and shoes. Includes a feature for searching by topic or by material. Consider what supplies or recycled materials have already been collected or could easily be collected for the makerspace and do a search.

Upcycle That—http://www.upcyclethat.com/   Upcycle That promises to share the best the web has to offer on upcycling ideas. They also produce and share some of their own creations. Stories and news about upcyclers and their projects are included. Projects are searchable by final product created ("make that") or materials utilized ("use that").

Velleman®, Inc.—http://www.vellemanusa.com/   Velleman produces such fun gadgets as flashing LED units, crawling microbug robots, voice changer, and other circuit board mini-kits. Velleman products may be bought through local hobby stores or purchased through online vendors.

Appendix 4: Maker Communities and Resources

A successful makerspace is strengthened by staying connected to the local and virtual community of the makers. The individuals and organizations stand by a firm philosophical belief in contributing and sharing knowledge and experiences. This is also a key connection to STEM and AASL's Learning4Life. Through contributing to the communal knowledge base, students meet AASL's national share and grow standards and fulfill the true maker philosophy of contributing to the community.

DIY—https://diy.org   At DIY, young makers can share projects, complete challenges, and earn skills patches, or badges. It features an A-to-Z list of maker categories, ranging from animator to zoologist. It offers young makers an opportunity to learn the basic skills and knowledge of the subject through learning and completing tasks, called challenges. Each subject includes a description, badge to earn for completing a certain number of challenges in that area, list of tools needed, and review of other subjects which are similar and might also interest the learner. Challenges include learning, and learning is accomplished through reading, watching, and doing.

Hackerspaces—http://hackerspaces.org   Hackerspaces is an international community of local hackerspaces, organizations, projects, and events. Important to library makerspaces is the education resource for training and education links, blogs, and tutorials. Prepare to be wowed by the thinking and doing in the adult hackerspace world.

iFixit—http://www.ifixit.com/ and http://ifixit.org   iFixit is the modern man's tinkerer and environmentalist. With a firm belief that repair is the truest form of recycling and is better than wasteful discard, iFixit pride themselves on taking apart modern gadgets to learn about how they work. From what is learned, a free repair manual with visual step-by-step instructions is created. There are manuals for a range of technologies including cameras, cell phones, game systems, household items, iPhone/iPod/iPad, Mac, media players, PCs, and vehicles. Levels of badges can be earned as a Community Contributor, Eco Role Model, and Heroic Citizen. Participation in making of the manuals is encouraged, including adding summaries, fixing guides, improving photos, and helping construct guides not yet created.

Library Makers—http://librarymakers.blogspot.ca   A blog out of Madison, Wisconsin, dedicated to hands-on learning in the library setting. Posted categories include craft, needlework, thinking (called Wonderworks), and toddler arts. Each event includes images of completed projects, links to other possible activities, and related books.

Make **Magazine**—http://makezine.com/   *Make* magazine, the companion website, and Maker Faires are all produced by Maker Media and is the leading maker magazine. Included are crafts, technology, sciences, projects, reviews of makerspace products (much like librarians are used to seeing for books), resources, technology, family connection, and much more. Subscription to the e-newsletter promises exclusive discounts and news.

Maker Camp—http://makezine.com/maker-camp   Attendees from throughout the world attend virtual maker workshops broadcast live via the web during the week of "camp." Much like a conference, attendees select sessions of interest to attend—a valuable way to expand makerspace knowledge without accruing travel expenses. Participate from the comfort of your own home or office computer through Google+.

Maker Librarian—http://www.makerlibrarian.com   Hosted by a librarian out of Canada, the Maker Librarian is a resource to assist librarians in learning and participating in the make movement.

MakerBot Thingiverse—http://www.thingiverse.com   A place for digital design and fabrication sharing. With a library of more than thirty thousand maker things, including 3D printing, art, fashion, hobbies, models, toys, and games, there is much to see, do, learn, and try.

Makerspace—http://makerspace.com   Makerspace is an online sharing community which includes a community blog, directory of Makerspaces and their websites, resources, a forum, and the official *Makerspace Playbook*. Makerspace also has a presence on Facebook and Google+. Makers share ideas, news, successes, and images. Join the mailing list to receive news, notices, and idea updates.

MAYker Monday—http://pcsweeney.com/2013/02/11/introducing-library-maykermondays   In what is hoped to be an annual event, Librarian Blogger PC Sweeney encourages librarians of all types to participate in MAYker Monday. Every Monday during the month of May, libraries are encouraged to host maker programming, training, or staff planning meetings. Included in this concept is the Maker CookBook where libraries are encouraged to add their ideas to the recipe book of library maker events and activities. Scroll down to find the hyperlink to the maker cookbook.

Mentor Makerspace—http://mentor.makerspace.com   A community built just for schools and teachers. Included is information about Young Makers, and how to host your own mini–Maker Faire. Symbolic of the maker philosophy, this website is evolving and continually under construction. It is sponsored by O'Reilly Media and Otherlab. Subscribe to the newsletter for updates and news.

MIT Media Labs: High-Low Tech Group—http://hlt.media.mit.edu/   MIT Media Lab website includes a list of recommended readings (publications), and comprehensive tutorials. Materials are subgrouped and linked to further information from vendors and suppliers. MIT Media Labs webcasts are hosted and archived at http://www.media.mit.edu/events/webcasts.

TechShop™—http://www.techshop.ws/   Brick and mortar maker shops throughout the country with intent to expand to more locations. In a similar format as a community art center, each TechShop hosts safety courses, classes, and provides access to cutting edge tech, hobby and craft tools, and heavy machinery for participants.

YoungMakers.org—http://youngmakers.org   The goal of Young Makers is to create a group of young makers who come together with mentors to think, experiment, invent, and create at fabrication facilities and exhibit successful makes at events.

Bibliography

American Library Association. "AASL Standards for the 21st-Century Learner." Last modified November 8, 2006. http://www.ala.org/aasl/standards-guidelines/learning-standards. Document ID: ec710ea2-99a2-27d4-b987-e042c9f4bf3f

American Library Association. "Learning4Life." Last modified September 6, 2012. Accessed February 17, 2013. http://www.ala.org/aasl/learning4life. Document ID: 04376c42-4519 -56f4-91e5-74a8553d5320

Anderson, Chris. *Makers: The New Industrial Revolution*. New York: Crown Business, 2012.

Britton, Lauren. "A Fabulous Laboratory." *Public Libraries*, July/August 2012: 30-33.

Brown, Stephen. "John Seely Brown on Motivating Learners." *Big Thinkers Series*. Recorded March 6, 2013. The Pearson Foundation. http://www.edutopia.org/john-seely -brown-motivating-learners-video?utm_source=facebook&utm_medium=pos&utm _campaign=video-seelytinker.

Duncan, Arne. U.S. Department of Education, "Digital Badges for Learning: Remarks by Secretary Duncan at 4th Annual Launch of the MacArthur Foundation Digital Media and Lifelong Learning Competition." Last modified September 15, 2011. http://www.ed.gov/news/ speeches/digital-badges-learning.

Homer. *The Odyssey*. Project Gutenberg, 2002. eBook.

"How to design breakthrough inventions." *60 Minutes*. Recorded January 6, 2013. CBS Interactive. http://www.cbsnews.com/video/watch/?id=50138327n.

Makerspace Team. "Makerspace Playbook DRAFT." makerspace.com. April 2012. http://maker spacedotcom.files.wordpress.com/2012/04/makerspaceplaybook-201204.pdf.

Merriam-Webster's Dictionary and Thesaurus. Springfield: Merriam-Webster, Incorporated, 2006. s.v. "Mentor."

National Governors Association Center for Best Practices, Council of Chief State School Officers. "Common Core State Standards for English Language Arts & Literacy in History/ Social Studies, Science, and Technical Subjects." 2010. http://www.corestandards.org/assets /CCSSI_ELA Standards.pdf.

National Governors Association Center for Best Practices, Council of Chief State School Officers. "Common Core Standards for Mathematics." 2010. http://www.corestandards.org /assets/CCSSI_Math Standards.pdf.

O'Duinn, Fiacre. *Maker Librarian*. 2013. http://www.makerlibrarian.com/ Accessed February 17, 2013.

Stansbury, Meris. "Digital Badges Could Help Measure 21st-Century Skills." *eSchool News*. October 11, 2011. http://www.eschoolnews.com/2011/10/11/digital-badges-could-help -measure-21st-century-skills/

Index

About the Author

LESLIE B. PREDDY has been the school librarian at Perry Meridian Middle School in Indianapolis, Indiana, since 1992. She is a past recipient of AASL's Collaborative School Library Media Award and School Library Media Program of the Year. She is a former MSD of Perry Township Teacher of the year and a 2010 finalist for Indiana State Teacher of the Year. She is a past president for the Association of Indiana School Library Educators (AISLE), a past general chair of the state's Young Hoosier Book Award (YHBA) program, and recipient of AISLE's prestigious Peggy L. Pfeiffer Service Award. She has published a variety of articles in professional journals and co-created online resources, and has served as an adjunct professor for Indiana University, Indiana State University, and IUPUI. Her book, *SSR with Intervention: A School Library Action Research Project* (Libraries Unlimited 2007) was named one of the Best Professional Books of 2007 by *Teacher Librarian*, and her book, *Social Readers: Promoting Reading in the 21st Century* (Libraries Unlimited 2010), was highly recommended by *Library Media Connection.*

Made in the USA
Middletown, DE
21 February 2015